Leading Your Church in EVANGELISM

Lewis A. Drummond

BROADMAN PRESS • Nashville, Tennessee

4262-10
ISBN: 0-8054-6210-4

First published by Marshall, Morgan & Scott, London, England,
with the title *Evangelism—The Counter-Revolution*

Dewey Decimal Classification: 269.2
Library of Congress Catalog Card Number: 75-30135
Printed in the United States of America

This book is affectionately dedicated to

MY WIFE

who has been the kind of minister's
wife
I have needed to carry out my life of
service for our
Lord Jesus Christ.

PREFACE

There is perhaps no theme that has captured the interest and imagination of the contemporary church quite as profoundly as the concept of evangelism. That which was once ignored or even ridiculed by many has now become the concern of most enlightened Christians. And although it may be true that some of the motives that have spurred this new impetus are not as high or spiritual as one would wish, none the less, evangelism is of vital interest to most Christians today and for that we must be grateful.

The purpose of this volume is to place in the hands of the pastor and Christian leader a basic work on the essential aspects of the evangelistic enterprise and to provide foundational guidelines on how to evangelize in a local church. It thus has a practical as well as a theological purpose. The primary theme of the book is that the pastor stands at the fountainhead of the evangelistic tide in a church. He holds the key to successful outreach. He, therefore, must become a "pastor-evangelist" in a deep and profound sense. Elucidating this essential truth, the book then attempts to guide the pastor and his church into a dynamic evangelistic program.

I must not close this brief preface without expressing my gratitude to those whose help has been invaluable.

Dr. James D. Williams of the Southwestern Baptist Theological Seminary in Fort Worth, Texas read the manuscript and made extremely helpful suggestions. To the faithful secretaries at Southern Baptist Theological Seminary who typed the manuscript, I acknowledge my debt. So I present my concept of the church's evangelistic task with the prayer that God will use it to inspire and help us all to "do the work of an evangelist" (2 Tim. 4:5).

CONTENTS

Bible Translations Used

NEB	*The New English Bible,* © The Delegates of the Oxford University Press and the Syndics of the Cambridge University Press, 1961, 1970. Used by permission.
RSV	Revised Standard Version. © Division of Christian education of the National Council of Churches in the United States of America, 1946, 1952.
Weymouth	*The New Testament in Modern Speech.* Boston: Pilgrim Press, 1903.

1 The Role of the Pastor in Evangelism

Every American is familiar with Washington Irving's intriguing little tale, *Rip Van Winkle.* Though it was written over 150 years ago, it has a startling relevance for the church today. You will remember that Rip had been slumbering away on a grassy knoll in the Catskill Mountains for twenty years, during which time the thirteen British colonies had become the thirteen, newly-formed United States of America. Poor old Rip had slept through the Revolution—and there is the story's relevance for us.

The fact that the church today is living and attempting to minister in a revolutionary atmosphere should be obvious to all. Everything seems to be in a state of radical change. All aspects of society are in flux. Foundations long accepted as valid are being shaken. No segment of the so-called Establishment escapes questioning. The only certainty appears to be that nothing will ever be quite the same again. But the most disquieting element of this sociological revolution is that often the "sleeping Rip Van Winkle" of the hour is none other than the church. Christians, who should be on the very cutting edge of this changing scene and moving society towards God, are often found slumbering away on some grassy knoll of irrelevance or unrealistic traditionalism while the world all but explodes and fragments around them.

In the light of such a situation it is, therefore, vital for the church to come alive to the contemporary sociological atmosphere and address itself to the problems this social revolution precipitates. I do not mean by this that the church is absolutely dead and thus ready for a decent burial—as some critics advocate. Rather, it more or less finds itself, at least in some of its institutionalized forms, in the grip of irrelevancy and needs to be awakened and updated. And if God's people can be shaken from their slumbers and made to see and respond to the tremendous evangelistic challenge of this turbulent hour, great things can be done. Moreover, it may just be that the disturbing voices being heard in our world today will be used to awaken the sleepers.

Contemporary Voices

A voice that is being currently heard loud and clear by the masses is that of a *secular scientism* with its purely empirical, rational approach to all of life. Those who advocate this line see truth and reality in only those things which the five senses and rationalism can verify. Strangely, even many contemporary philosophers have enrolled in this school. The result is that the great and vitally important metaphysical questions that philosophy has always grappled with are now banned from discussion. These thinkers take this rigid empirical line because metaphysical contemplation raises questions, the answers to which are not verifiable rationally or empirically; therefore, they are to be rejected. Most university philosophical departments in Europe and America are more or less committed to some form of linguistic, empirical thought. The result is that philosophy has suffered correspondingly as it has ignored many vital issues. Moreover, it seems abundantly clear that the average man in the street shares in the attitude, even if in an unsophisticated way. He is more often than not a mere pragmatic empiricist that rejects as meaningless the great spiritual realities of life; hence, our American obsession with the materialistic, affluent society. Both the professional philosopher and the common man alike all but worship at the shrine of a scientific approach to truth, meaning, and reality.

No one wishes to decry the amazing advance and benefit that scientific, empirical investigation has produced. We enjoy, and rightly so, the good things of the affluent society. But many have built their entire system of *values* on this level, and this is where the problems begin. Ignoring the reality of spiritual values, they define security on a purely materialistic basis. Health and wholeness are sought in scientific medicine and behavioristic psychology alone. Status, and therefore acceptance by one's peers, means the attainment of economic levels. In the spirit of Hegel, who claimed everything for his pure rationalism, these devotees of empirical science believe that all problems, in principle if not yet in fact, can finally be solved in the laboratory or on the psychiatrist's couch. Though the common man may not be able, as the philosopher can, to present a formal rationale for his completely empirical, rational approach to reality, he certainly lives out on a practical level those basic presuppositions.

The pressing problem for evangelism that this situation precipitates is that the church must find a convincing apologetic for our faith in this empirical and rationalistic scientific atmosphere. For example, the so-called conflict between science and religion that has caused many young people to cast their vote for the laboratory instead of the pulpit must be resolved. And it cannot be done by arguing on the level that many Christians do today, namely, never getting down to the essential presuppositions of what truth is. Schaeffer has correctly pointed out:

> The floodwaters of secular thought . . . overwhelmed the church because the leaders did not understand the importance of combating a false set of presuppositions. They largely fought the battle on the wrong ground and so, instead of being far ahead in both defence and communication, they lagged woefully behind. . . . Man thinks differently concerning truth, and so now for us, more than ever before, a presuppositional apologetic is imperative.[1]

The place of apologetics in evangelism is, of course, a subject in itself and can scarcely be debated in this limited space. What is essential to see is that unless we can help the present and especially the next generation—which is, as never before, a "thinking" generation—to find a resolution to the supposed antithesis between empirical rationalism and the Christian faith, we shall lose many for Christ and his church. This issue was brought home to me quite forcefully recently. I led in a student campaign in one of the large universities in Kentucky. I asked the student religious minister how many of the student body were affiliated with my own particular denomination. His answer was 2,000. I asked how many were involved in the local churches in the city. His startling reply was 125. It seems we lose almost 90 percent of our young people when they go off to college and for the first time are faced with a real need for a convincing apologetic for their faith and discover they have none. To this issue the local church *must* be awakened. Pastors and youth leaders must come alive to the almost unbelievable falling away of university students and help prepare young people for what they will encounter when they leave the shelter of the home church and face the university situation.

Another voice being heard today is somewhat in contrast to the appeal of empirical science. This voice can probably be called, because a label is convenient, *agnostic existentialism.* The existentialist, in over-simplified terms, sees existence as more important than essence. So one is urged to find reality and meaning in one's human experience. Drain from each moment of existence all the good it has to offer. It is what "turns you on" that matters. Objective standards are passé. It is "inner truth" where meaning is found. This line of thought, rather than leading to a kind of proud utopianism and optimism as scientific empiricism tends to do, leads many to a serious and almost morbid despair. They discover that the chaos of this world seems to present a universe with no ultimate reality, order, or meaning. And because they fail to look beyond the immediacy of their temporal existence, deep despair can easily ensue. Still, the practical result of this orientation to life is in essence the same as for the hard-nosed empiricist, namely, no God. As Heidegger has expressed it, we came from nothing and we go to nothing. One is thus constantly thrown back on his own self. It may be that not all who live in this general frame of reference are propositional atheists. Yet they are something of a practical atheist as far as everyday living is concerned.

At the same time, these advocates have rejected philosophical rationalism, and in a modified sense even empiricism, as a way to truth and meaning. The crunch for the church is, they also reject the concept of revealed truth which is clearly the Christian position. So with little or nothing left to build upon except their own selves, they just opt out. This is their decision of "courage" in order to become an "authentic self."

As is evident, here is where we find many young people and young adults today; whether they be of the general mindset of the "revolutionary sixties" or the strange "passive seventies." Granted that many of them have not thought out their position in philosophical terms, this is still their basic approach to life. And if the church thinks them to be just long-haired, immoral, and reactionary and should thus be held up to scorn and contempt, it is going to miss evangelizing a very important segment of society. A cursory survey of almost every facet of contemporary life should tell us this. Existential philosophy is almost dominating the field of modern music, the arts, the theater, television, advertising, etc. Few of the young set are free from its influence. They all read Camus, Sartre, and others. They all love the rock music of the groups. They all "dig" modern art. We who would evangelize must come to grips with this tremendously influential issue that has precipitated so many subcultures, e.g. the drug scene, the sex scene, transcendental meditation, *ad infinitum*.

A third voice that presently sallies forth is *humanism*, i.e. the concept which holds that life is to be understood in purely human terms. There have always been humanists, but they have usually tended to stay in their ivory towers or in relatively small, esoteric groups. Perhaps the reason humanism as an orientation to life has come down to the marketplace in this generation is in some sense because of the influence of behavioristic psychology. Probably the influence of behaviorism was essentially negative in that it eliminated for many the relevance, if not the concept, of God. But this movement coupled with the industrial revolution and its depersonalization of man caused the human character to cry out desperately for recognition. So today we have a sort of romantic materialistic view of human personality. Growing out of this basic approach to existence, humanism says that all that is real and of ultimate value are the human personality and human interests. This has clearly been a growing life view, especially since Freud. As is the case with scientism and existentialism, there is an element of truth in humanism. All Christians should find sympathy with philanthropical endeavors to enhance human dignity and meet the pressing needs of our fellowmen. Persons are important, vitally important. But when materialistic humanism becomes a world view that excludes God and spiritual values as the ultimate good and romanticizes about man and his accomplishments, that is when trouble begins for the evangel. This is one of the current life views with which the church must cope.

Perhaps the most disturbing issue to the average Christian is the strange milieu in which contemporary ethics finds itself. This is largely due, I believe, to the present day spirit of *relativism,* i.e. the idea that there are no such things as absolutes. This basic presupposition has all but taken the hour. Even the traditional systems of logic and truth have fallen. As we know, the first move in classical logical thought is: if you have "A," it is not "Non-A." But as Schaeffer says, "if you understand the extent to which this no longer holds sway, you will understand our present situation." [2] Everything is relative; there are no absolutes, we are told. Ernest Hemingway expressed it like this: "What is moral is what you feel good after. What is evil is what you feel bad after." In other words, there are no absolute ethical or moral principles. It is in something of this atmosphere that the so-called situation ethic emerged with its rejection of absolute standards. As young people are urged to "do their thing," established principles of moral right and wrong are rejected. As Harvey Cox has advocated in more philosophical terms, "There is no reason that man must believe the ethical standards he lives by came down from heaven inscribed on golden tablets. He can accept the fact that value systems, like states and civilizations, come and go. They are conditioned by their history and claim no finality." [3]

It is obvious that certain Victorian concepts needed to fall. But because of the spirit of relativism in ethics, many of the great biblical principles of moral right have been swept away in the avalanche. In the light of this disappearance of objective, securely grounded values, it is little wonder that Tillich called this world a "land of broken symbols." The consequence of it all is that today there is such confusion in ethics that everyone seems to be in a state of moral turmoil, from the thinker in his isolated study to the hippie in his communal group. If ever an age were ethically and morally adrift on a sea of uncertainty, this is that age.

Another strange aspect of the moral confusion of the moment is found in the fact that, generally speaking, those over forty see morals and ethics on more of an individual basis while the younger generation sees them on a larger social level. For example, older adults tend to hold in contempt young people who advocate a very worthy moral social issue, because after the discussion the young people may go to bed together. By the same token, young people display contempt for the older view of sexual morality because many of its advocates are seemingly blind to the pressing moral social issues that have *them* "turned on." As a result, both groups become rather lop-sided in their ethical concepts, for they fail to see that morals are both individual and social. Thus the so-called generation gap widens. And tragically, the church seems less able to evangelize as this gap becomes wider.

Our day of ferment can perhaps best be summarized and described with that much used and confused word *secularism*. It is simply that many people are living today as if God were dead even though they may deny the concepts of the radical thinkers. And I would suppose that the average secularized man has a bit of all these current philosophies in his life view. There are few purists today. If Socrates was right when he said, "The unexamined life is not worth living," Mr. Average Man is living a pretty worthless life. Few have thought out in a systematic way their life-style—they just live it. Most people are just pragmatists. If a thing or thought works, they uncritically utilize it. The results are that the bulk of people live a simple, practical, secular life.

The deeply disturbing result of all this milieu in which people are trying to find meaning and value is that men, wherever they may turn, are faced with their "lostness." Lost to real purpose in life, lost to meaningful relationships, lost to themselves, *lost to God*, they merely float about on the turbulent sea of circumstances and conflicting ideologies, never able to settle in any port and discover reality. It is dramatically true that without Jesus Christ, man is lost, empty, estranged, and quite hopeless. Adrift on his secular sea, he desperately needs to find anchor in Jesus Christ. It is as true in the twentieth century as in the first; apart from a saving relationship to God through Jesus Christ, secular man is profoundly and eternally lost. He above all needs to find God and be redeemed from his empty, secular life. And it is the responsibility of the Christian community to direct him towards the way to life that has meaning. That is the church's prime ministry—not its only one to be sure, but its prime task.

Strange Reactions

This secular society has been met with widely divergent reactions within the thinking Christian community. There are those who see any sort of human emancipation as a threat to their dogmatically closed and extremely narrow world view. Surely this reaction is not the biblical answer and, therefore, is no answer at all. Conversely, there are those who herald this day as the day of liberation from old erroneous forms whose demise is long overdue. Society has at last "come of age," they tell us. Thus, a secularization theology emerged a few years ago which advocates the rejection of any closed world view, especially a closed theological world view. As Harvey Cox has said, defining secularization theology, "It is the loosing of the world from religious and quasi-religious understandings of itself, the dispelling of all closed world-views, the breaking of all supernatural myths and sacred symbols. . . . It has relativized religious world views and thus rendered them innocuous." [4]

Such a position leaves one a bit uneasy in that several questions come to mind:

1. Is the presupposition (for it is a presupposition) that a closed world view is untenable a valid position? This is highly debatable.

2. Does not the Bible present what Cox calls a "closed world view"? His arguments to the contrary are hardly convincing. (Cox's biblical exegesis seems woefully inadequate.)

3. Can one ever have any sort of tenable cosmology without its being something of a closed world view?

Be that as it may, it seems clear that a purely secularization theology, despite its admirable aspects, is not the biblical view in the truest sense and consequently will not give any lasting, satisfying answers to today's utter secularism. We shall be discussing this type of liberal "new theology" in more detail later. Suffice it to say here that I hold that secularization theology will not bring secular man back to God in the biblical sense of what it means to be redeemed. The reason I take this position is because I feel that these theologians fail to supply adequate answers to the basic questions men are asking this hour, namely "Who am I?" and "Where am I going?"

Now it is in this atmosphere that the church is called upon to minister today. And the two basic questions cited above are what we are being asked by contemporary man in his lostness. The task of the church is to present Christ to the world as we find it, not as it was or as we would like it, and to communicate in a relevant manner that in Christ alone is to be found the answer to life's ultimate questions.

Here is where the trouble begins, for it is clear that many churches have failed to some extent in their evangelistic responsibility. Moreover, it seems that this relative ineffectiveness to communicate the gospel relevantly to a rapidly changing world is a growing problem. This can be seen to a greater or lesser degree in the boycott of the institutionalized church by certain segments of society. It is true that there is a general disillusionment with all institutions and an overall questioning of everything that smacks of the Establishment. The churches have had to share in this spirit. As pointed out by Paul Musselman, "The dying urban churches are indications of an unplanned, but nevertheless real protest by the urban disinherited. The streams of people who pass but never enter an urban church represents a form of unconscious picketing against the church." [5] But this disillusionment with institutionalism is not the only reason that people bypass the churches today. And it surely cannot be used as an "out" to excuse our lack of effective evangelism. There are many other reasons, and two of these cannot be disregarded for we can do something constructive about them. These issues must be met courageously.

Two Issues to Face

First, there is the church's reluctance to change and to speak relevantly to our day. Let me illustrate this problematic attitude. Not long ago I was conducting a session on the theme of effective local church evangelism. The participants came from different churches and consisted largely of laymen. I was advocating changes in programs and procedures that would aid in more effectively reaching people with the gospel. During the discussion period that followed a layman suddenly burst out, "What's wrong with meeting at eleven o'clock on Sunday morning for worship?" I did not recall the hour of worship even being mentioned in our discussion concerning change. Here was a man so bound to a specific program as he had known it that he was almost angered at the thought of *any* change, even one as minor as that and even if it meant ministering more effectively.

But this attitude is not restricted to the layman. I was speaking to a group of ministers recently. In the course of the discussion that followed my address on pastoral evangelism and the need to update evangelistic methodology, I mentioned that much of what the Victorian era implied is rejected by many today. One minister rose to say that he did not concur with that line of thought at all. He felt most people still loved Victoriana as was indicated by their willingness to buy Victorian antiques. Of course, he did not realize the reason that Victorian antiques are popular is because they are plentiful and cheap. The tragedy was, however, here was a minister whose whole spirit implied that old methodologies must be kept regardless of their inadequacies. It was quite disturbing to sense how far he was removed from the realities and necessities of the day. Remember, the seven last words of the church are, "We haven't done it that way before!" If *anyone* should be alive to the contemporary scene and be ready for change, it should be ministers.

When one speaks of the necessity for overturning traditions, the reference is essentially to outmoded methodologies. The great traditions and theologies of Christianity must remain. The gospel itself is always unchanging. But every generation has the right to hear the good news communicated in a fashion that addresses its message in current forms and to man in his present sociological environment. For us today this implies change—often drastic change—in our methods and programs. Georgia Harkness has rightly said, "If the church is to win the battle against secularism by the sword of the Spirit, some deep-seated changes are in order." [6] We can no longer conduct business as usual. The business is the same, but conducting it as usual can spell death to congregations, not to say what happens to the multitudes without Christ. It is as simple as that. I know that this issue has been discussed *ad nauseum*. But the time for discussion is over. Courageous action is now demanded. If we are in any way to meet the demands of this revolutionary age, something of a counter-revolution must take place within the churches. And we can change significantly if we will. I would hope that some practical suggestions and guidelines will be found in these pages that will enable us to get started. But more of that later.

Secondly, there is another impediment to the church's evangelistic ministry today. It centers in the somewhat "uncertain sound" that some preachers and churches have trumpeted. This is bewildering to people. The man in the street hears what is called the church's message, and because of the diversity of "gospels" he may hear, he does not know what to believe. He thus loses confidence in the church's claim to speak God's truth and proceeds to do "what is right (or wrong) in his own eyes." What is the gospel then? What is our message? It is that which is implied by the term *kerygma*. We shall discuss the theology of the *kerygma* in a subsequent chapter. May I simply summarize here and say the church has only one clear note to sound to all, namely "Christ and him crucified" (1 Cor. 2:2). This is our good news. When this truth is heralded, men hear. It is true that we cannot dictate what others proclaim. But we can be sure that our message is that which men need most to understand. Our evangelism will never be successful or relevant until we declare Christ. This issue we must face. In the light of this central truth, here is a good place to raise the key question.

What Is Evangelism?

Various writers have used the terms *evangelism* or its counterpart *mission* rather fast and loose. To this point, I have used them quite freely. But a precise definition is important. In attempting to give a sound meaning to the words, an Anglican commission on evangelism said, "To evangelize is so to present Christ Jesus in the power of the Holy Spirit that men shall come to put their trust in God through Him, to accept Him as their Saviour, and serve Him as their King in the fellowship of His Church." [7] W. E. Sangster, the great British Methodist preacher, tells us that "evangelism is going to the people outside. It is the proclamation of the good news of God in Jesus Christ to 'them that are without'. . . . It is the sheer work of the Herald who goes in the name of the King to the people who, either openly or by their indifference, deny their allegiance to their rightful Lord. He blows the trumpet and demands to be heard." [8] Professor Schilling of Boston University states: "Evangelism is the proclamation, in word or deed, of the 'good news of Jesus Christ' with the aim of winning a positive response. It is the endeavor to bring persons whole-heartedly to accept and live by the redemptive love of God as revealed in Jesus Christ." [9] Douglas Webster points out in general terms that "evangelism is the proclamation of the gospel." [10] And we all know the pungent definition of D. T. Niles that evangelism is simply "one beggar telling another beggar where to find bread."

Perhaps the concept can be summarized and conveyed in this fashion: Evangelism is a concerted effort to confront the unbeliever with the truth about and claims of Jesus Christ and to challenge him with the view of leading him into repentance toward God and faith in our Lord Jesus Christ and, thus, into the fellowship of the church.

If we will grant that these definitions are valid from a biblical perspective, it is clear that the term *evangelism* is used by many today in too broad a sense and by others in too narrow a manner. For example, evangelism is simply not everything we do, as some seem to understand it. Although the spirit of evangelism should permeate all Christian activity and ministry, everything we do is not evangelism *per se.* It can be rather self-deceptive to define evangelism too broadly. It can even be a subtle excuse for not engaging in outright, pointed evangelistic endeavors. Conversely, evangelism is surely more than just formally "preaching the gospel." Communicating the good news is a much broader concept than doing no more than what the preacher does from the pulpit. It clearly implies action as well as proclamation. And the entire church is to engage in it.

So there is our task: to evangelize a bewildered mass, caught up in a sociological, ethical, ecological, philosophical revolution that has all but overturned every stabilizing tradition. And we have surely found by now that "we are heading for sure disaster in the church of our contemporary society when we insist on forcing new wine into old wineskins".[11] A new day is upon us and, therefore, a new challenge is before us. What a challenge it is! Will we win the day for Christ? That is the most pressing question we face. I for one believe the church still has a real measure of vitality, and I surely believe God can do mighty things—and do those things through his people. We can evangelize our world in our generation if the church can be renewed and committed to the task. But to see this desperately needed renewal and a new dynamic impetus for outreach, it is essential that we must first come to grips with our theology. That is really where it all starts.

The Concept of Church-centered Evangelism

It is axiomatic that the first principle of church-centered evangelism is that outreach is the church's primary mission in the world. Of course, this does not state the case quite properly. The mission is actually God's mission. The church merely shares in the *missio Dei*, as it has been called. But in this secondary sense the church does have a calling and it has been commissioned to the task by our Lord himself. Surely all would agree that Jesus' statement in Matthew 28:19-20 is foundational to the very life and ministry of the church, and these words are clearly the words of evangelism: "Go forth therefore and make all nations my disciples; baptize men everywhere in the name of the Father and the Son and the Holy Spirit, and teach them to observe all that I have commanded you. And be assured, I am with you always, to the end of time" (NEB). Thus the church shares in the *missio Dei* and in so doing lives close to the heart of God. It would seem today that no apologetic is needed to convince the knowledgeable Christian and pastor that mission is the core of the local church's ministry. On the contrary, evangelism and its study has become one of the contemporary church's keenest interests.

Simply put then, God is the Divine Missionary, i.e. God is on a mission of world redemption. And his basic plan for world evangelization is the use of the instrumentality of the church. This is why it is so clear in the Scriptures that, as Whitesell tells us, "New Testament local churches were nerve centers of evangelism, and in this respect constitute a pattern for local churches of all ages. Missionary evangelism had produced these local churches, and they in turn made evangelism and missionary activity their main business." [12]

Pastors and laymen with insight have long recognized this theological truth. Yet it appears that the church as a whole has failed to grasp in depth the importance and reality of its call to mission, at least in a practical sense. Surely it is God's expectation that the entire church be involved in the task. As Leighton Ford has said, "If our goal is the penetration of the whole world; then for the agents to carry out the task we must aim at nothing less than the mobilization of the whole church." [13] What then will fully awaken the whole church from its dogmatic and traditional slumbers and motivate it to fulfill its ministry? How will the average layman be motivated? That is the issue.

We shall discuss the problem of apathy in more detail later, but it can be repeated again that it would obviously help if the church could come alive to the upheaval society is undergoing. This is why several pages were given to a diagnosis of this scene. It seems rather strange that the church, which is itself a real part of society and to some extent shares in the revolution, has developed something of a retreating ghetto mentality. But until the church is aware of the comtemporary scene and realizes that it is to minister in a preserving capacity in the real world, it will find extreme difficulty in becoming the "church for others." As the report of the Western European Working Group of the Department on Studies in Evangelism aptly pointed out:

> Faced with secular society, with the understanding of history as involving constant change and transformation and with the acknowledgement that the Church has to turn itself outwards to the world, we are summoned in the present age, as in any age, to test the traditions of the churches and their own self-understanding.
>
> One may say we are in danger of perpetuating "come-structures" instead of replacing them by "go-structures". One may say that inertia has replaced the dynamism of the Gospel and of participation in the mission of God. . . . Because of this inertia and this insulation from the world, we have come to exist beside and often outside the reality of the world, instead of being present in its structures. Our own structures then operate as obstacles and hindrances preventing the proclamation of the Gospel from reaching mankind.[14]

Yet regardless of the present problems within and without, we have learned that it is the church that God basically uses to accomplish the task. This has invariably been the divine plan, and I suppose always will be. With its often archaic structures, its apathy, its reluctance to change, and its thousand and one other difficulties, the church still remains as the one to "stand in the gap" and minister Christ to the world.* Further, as I have already implied, I do not share the despair that some feel for the contemporary church. I believe the Western European Working Group was correct when it emphasized that part of the mission of the church is to renew

---

*However, when we make such a claim for the church, let it be understood that this does not imply that God is at work only in and through the structures of the church's current institutional forms. God is obviously working in the world in a thousand different ways. We can surely see what God is doing by reading reports from various organizations that labor for the betterment of the human lot as well as by reading the annual reports of our various denominational agencies. We can even read the daily newspapers and see the hand of God as he ministers to human need through others than the church. This is one area of truth where the secularization theologians are challenging us. And we should give pause to thank God for all he is doing and for our becoming increasingly aware of it. Yet in the prime task of world evangelization, it is still the church that is the basic instrument of God.

itself. The Holy Spirit is constantly moving the church towards renewal and resurrection. And there are many signs that point in the direction of renewal: for instance, a fresh interest in evangelism everywhere, ministers gathering in conference and clinics on outreach, new thrusts for evangelism cropping out in various church structures, etc. All these things should encourage those committed to evangelism. Perhaps we are on the verge of a new worldwide gospel impact. To that end one would surely hope and pray.

A New Challenge Needed

Still, there are painful days ahead. The church is not going to be revolutionized inwardly so as to cope with the revolution outside until some forthright and courageous challenges are presented to it. And from what quarter will such a call and challenge come? It seems self-evident from what quarter it *should* come, namely, the pastor. It is most important for the informed layman as well as for the minister of the congregation to see that in a theology of church-centered evangelism, the pastor has the key role.

The Responsibility of the Pastor as Evangelist

This theme immediately brings to mind Paul's challenge to Timothy to "do the work of an evangelist, fulfill your ministry" (2 Tim. 4:5, RSV). The clear implication of this passage is that a pastor cannot fulfill his ministry unless he fulfills his role as evangelist. This certainly means far more than merely preaching evangelistic sermons from time to time, although that is a part of it. In the light of the Scriptures and in a day like today, it must mean leading the whole church to become an evangelistic and mission-minded body. Experience has surely taught us, as C. E. Autry puts it:

> The place of the pastor in the evangelism of the local church is strategic. If he is evangelistic, the church will ordinarily be evangelistic. The degree to which the pastor is evangelistic will be reflected in the church. If he is lukewarm, the church will very likely be lukewarm. If he is intensely evangelistic, the church will reflect the

warmth and concern of the pastor.[15]

It is evident that a local church eventually takes on the basic attitudes of its pastor. Yet this is as it should be if one's ministry is at all effective. I cannot express too forcefully this essential principle of the minister becoming in a true sense a pastor-evangelist. This is actually the theme of the entire book; for if a local church is to be an evangelistic church and geared to effective outreach, the pastor is normally the key man.

The Principle of the Pastor-evangelist

But is this really the pastor's role? Have I overstated the case? Perhaps we can find an answer to these questions in what the New Testament presents as the position of the pastor in a local congregation. It must first be recognized that today in all of our denominations we are probably not duplicating exactly the New Testament pattern concerning the ministry. For example, there was a plurality of elders or pastors which only the large contemporary churches have. Probably the bishop had a somewhat different role than the present-day bishop in those communions which still keep the office. The point is, however, that the New Testament words which are used to describe the various offices in the first-century church give us something of an insight into the function of today's pastor.

Look first at the word *presbyters* or *elders*. This term is essentially a title of dignity. The early church borrowed it from the Jewish community. Members of the honored Sanhedrin, for example, were often called elders. It seems that the Greeks used the term in a similar fashion before the Jews brought it into their vocabulary. The actual function of the dignified office of elder is found in the word *episkopoi* or *bishop*, which literally means "overseer." Thayer points out "that they (the elders) did not differ at all from the (*episkopoi*) bishop or overseer (as is acknowledged also by Jerome on Titus 1:5) . . . is evident from the fact that the two words are used indiscriminately. . . . The title *episkopos* denotes the function, *presbuteros* the dignity." [16]

These men were, as the terms imply, the governing body of the local church. They were charged with the task of leading the congregation into its proper life and ministry. Paul tells them the Holy Spirit had made them overseers (Acts 20:28), and they were "to shepherd" (*poimainein*) the church of God. But this office was not only one of authority—though it was that. In James we find them visiting and praying for the sick (Jas. 5:13-15). In 1 Timothy 5:17 the elders are to "labour in the word and doctrine" (KJV). Hebrews 13:7,17,24 (while another Greek word is used for the office of elder) states that those who rule are those who "spake unto you the word of God" and for the sake of the readers "watch in behalf of your souls." This combination of ruling with preaching, teaching, and pastoral responsibility is clearly in line with the entire New Testament concept of the ministry. Most keenly to be felt by the ministers was their responsibility to God for the welfare of the flock under their charge.

Another aspect of ministry is found in the Greek word *diakonoi* for "deacon." Although there seems to be a special group of men in the New Testament churches who were appointed to this particular office and ministry, the word is used at times interchangeably with the positions of elder, evangelist, or even apostle (e.g., 1 Cor. 3:5). It is well known that the word essentially means "service" or "ministering." And as we find again in Thayer it is often used in connection with those who, by God's command, promote and proclaim religion among men.[17] The prime impact of this word as it relates to the pastor, therefore, is that he is God's servant, ministering to God's people to promote the true faith of Christ.

One of the most interesting passages concerning the ministry in the New Testament church is that found in Ephesians 4:11-12: "And these were his gifts: some to be apostles, some prophets, some evangelists, some pastors and teachers, to equip God's people for work in his service, to the building up of the body of Christ" (NEB).

These verses clearly present the office-bearers of the first-century church. It is of interest initially because it gives us some insight into the organization and administrative structure of the early church. Barclay states from this Ephesian passage that there were actually three kinds of office-bearers in Paul's time. (1) There were those whose authority and word were universal, i.e. to the entire church. (2) There were also those whose ministry was not restricted to one place. They had a wandering or itinerant ministry. (3) Finally, there were those who ministered essentially to one congregation in one place.[18]

In the first category of ministry we find the apostles. This meant more than just the Twelve. For instance, Silvanus (1 Thess. 2:6), Andronicus and Junia (Rom. 16:7), and, of course, Paul and Barnabas were called apostles in the sense that the term is used in Ephesians 4. It was required that these men had seen the Lord and been a witness to his resurrection. In this historical sense, therefore, this specific office was to pass away. Yet in spirit, all true ministers are apostles, for they are the ones sent (*apostolos*) by God to bear witness to the resurrection.

The second group of ministers, the wanderers, are called prophets and evangelists. The prophet, as a forth-teller (more than a fore-teller) of God's truth, went about preaching in the power of the Spirit and was a man of great influence. Before long, this office seemed to vanish from the life of the early church. Perhaps there were those who abused the office so that it fell into some disrepute. The evangelists were probably what we today would call missionaries. They were the bringers of good news. They did not exercise the prestige or authority of the apostles; they did not have the early influence of the Spirit-inspired prophets; they were more or less the rank and file missionaries of the church who went about proclaiming the gospel.

Finally, there were the pastors-teachers. They were the more settled and permanent ministry in the local church. This office title seems to be a double phrase to describe one essential group of ministers. Their task is found in their title; they were to teach and preach, and the content of their message was the Christian faith. These men were more than simply teachers and preachers; they were also pastors (*poimenas*) or shepherds. They were to feed the flock of God (1 Pet. 5:2) and to care for and protect the sheep (Acts 20:28). Jesus Christ himself is the supreme example, for he is called the chief Shepherd (1 Pet. 5:4) and the Shepherd of all men's souls (1 Pet. 2:25). What a responsible position this was! As Barclay says, "The shepherd of the flock of God is the man who bears God's people on his heart, who feeds them with the truth, who seeks them when they stray away, and who defends them from all that would hurt or destroy or distort their faith." [19]

The impact of this Ephesian passage for our present purpose is not just to give us a picture of the New Testament structures of the ministry, interesting as that is. What is to be seen is that God gave these gifted men as his gifts to the church so that the church might be equipped to do the work of the ministry. As has already been emphasized, it is the whole church to whom the work of the ministry has been committed. The "ministers" or "clergymen" as we commonly call them, are given to the church to prepare the church to carry on its service. The impact of this well-known and much discussed principle in the field of evangelism is obvious. Having discovered that the prime ministry of the church is mission, the clear implication is that the real evangelists are the church members themselves. And the pastor is to equip the Christians under his charge for this vital task. This is surely the only conclusion that can be drawn from all that the New Testament says concerning the leader of a congregation and the role he is to fill relative to mission. He is a bishop, an overseer; he is an elder, a man of respect and honor; he is a deacon, a servant of the people; he is a pastor, one who feeds and guards the flock; he is a preacher and teacher to communicate the faith; he is an apostle, one sent by God; he is a prophet, one who speaks in the power of the Holy Spirit; he is an evangelist, one who heralds good news. This is something of the spirit of the pastor's role as he attempts to lead his flock with spiritual authority into fields of evangelistic ministry.

This is a fantastic order and no man can possibly possess all of these gifts to perfection. Yet it is surely implied that the pastor of a local congregation must assume the responsibility of leading and equipping the whole church to fulfill its ministry. It is to this position he has been called by the Holy Spirit. And regardless of how inadequate he may feel—or actually may be—to this work he must unreservedly give himself as best he can.

So here we are back to the previous theme: the entire church becoming mobilized and equipped to evangelize our revolutionary society. And it should be amply clear that the essential responsibility for this Herculean task of leading and equipping the church settles essentially on the shoulders of the pastor. This is the most vital aspect of what it means to be a pastor-evangelist. As stated by Whitesell:

> The Pastor-evangelist, then, is the key-man in local church evangelism, and local church evangelism is the key to all other evangelism. The pastor must lead his people in intercessory prayer for the lost; he must inspire them, teach them, organize them, send them out, and encourage them to continue in this greatest of all church work.[20]

This then is the pastor's task, and I think it is not put too strongly to say that if he fails in this obligation, he has missed a very vital part of his ministry.

Some Examples of Pastor-evangelists

History is not without its examples to reinforce the validity of this principle. Take the marvellous ministry of Richard Baxter of Kidderminster, England in the eighteenth century. Although he was pastor in a small town of only 5,000 and came to a very provincial and weak church, he was soon used to kindle a bright flame of evangelism. Baxter was an exceptionally powerful preacher; he "preached as a dying man to dying men," he said. It is also true that he did much personal evangelism himself in that he had every family in the community into his home. But these things were not the only reason for the effectiveness of his evangelistic outreach. Perhaps his greatest genius lay in the fact that he led his people to set up family worship in their homes where they themselves could communicate the Christian faith to their families and others. As a result of the remarkable work of Baxter as a pastor-evangelist it has been said that "Kidderminster became a veritable colony of heaven in an hour of general spiritual darkness and wickedness." [21]

Or look at the ministry of Charles Haddon Spurgeon in the last century. We all know he was a preacher *par excellence.* Still he devoted a large part of his ministry to the training of young men to go out and share Christ. Spurgeon once said, "He who converts a soul draws water from a fountain, but he who trains a soul-winner digs a well, from which thousands may drink to eternal life." And space precludes the interesting accounts of giants of the past who spent much time training "evangelists" to declare Christ: men like John Wesley, Charles Finney, Bernard of Clairvaux, Francis of Assisi, and a host of others.

It is when we come to the contemporary twentieth century that we can find perhaps the clearest examples of the pastor-evangelist at work. I have a personal friend who has excelled in his responsibility in this field. He started his work with two concerned laymen. He taught and encouraged them in the area of personal evangelism. These two men began to lead people to faith in Christ. Soon they recruited two more to join them in the work. Now four men were engaged. Soon there were eight as the work developed. Before long, some women were inspired, and they along with several young people gave themselves to the task. Soon a host of trained and zealous Christians were constantly witnessing. All the organizations of the church—the Sunday School, training classes, women's and men's work, etc.—have been caught up in the spirit of mission. The whole church throbs with evangelistic fervor. The consequences are that literally hundreds are reached for Christ and his church every year. It took time to be sure. There were painful days, and there are still problems. But here was a pastor who saw his role, took it seriously, and starting with only two men and working and visiting with them and training them for mission, became a pastor-evangelist in a most profound sense.

Another modern-day example can be seen in the dynamic and effective program of the Belmont Heights Baptist Church in Nashville, Tennessee. Here the pastor, Robert J. Norman, has led the church in a beautiful balance of social action and evangelistic involvement. The church carries on one of the finest ministries to meet people's temporal needs I know of. There are language classes for internationals, homemaking group studies, day care, recreational activities for all groups, and a host of other innovative ministries. In this fully integrated congregation, every community need is seen as an opportunity to share in Christ's name—and it is a community of varied needs in which the church is located. At the same time, a dynamic evangelistic outreach ministry goes on. The services are alive with fervor and power. Visitation is continually stressed. Training in witnessing is a vital part of the overall program along with various other means of reaching all classes of people for Christ. It is a beautiful picture of what the urban church in the twentieth century should be. And it all grew out of the pastor's deep commitment to be a pastor-evangelist in the true, broad sense of the word. He refused to be polarized between social action and evangelism.

We could cite many examples, but these make it quite clear that any church can come alive to its opportunity if the leadership—especially the pastor—will take up the challenge and lead the people of God into the kind of ministry the Spirit of God honors and blesses.

Now it may sound a bit idealistic to make such claims; many

may even feel it impossible to mobilize an entire congregation. I must admit that the ideal may never be perfectly realized. But regardless of the problems, the principle remains and the obligation must be faced by pastors.

In chapter 3 we shall be discussing this theme in far more detail and attempt to present some practical ideas wherein a beginning can perhaps be found. Be that as it may, the inevitable conclusion of all that has been said is quite simple logic. The major premise is that the evangelization of our turbulent, changing world rests upon the gearing and equipping of the whole body of Christ to engage in the *missio Dei.* The minor premise is that this mobilization and equipping task is essentially the responsibility of the pastor in the local congregation. The conclusion can only be that if the mission is significantly successful, the pastor must rise to the challenge of his role. If he fails to do so and refuses to become in a very profound sense a pastor-evangelist, the church will suffer. But if he does accept his place in the economy of God, I am convinced the church can rise from her slumbers and pick up the challenge of the hour. This is the counter-revolution I am calling for. If the challenge is met, the last decades of this century could well see a new and relevant thrust for evangelism that it has not seen for many years.

Notes

1. Francis Schaeffer, *The God Who is There* (London: Hodder and Stoughton, 1968, p. 15.
2. Ibid., p. 14.
3. Harvey Cox, *The Secular City* (New York: Macmillan Company, 1965), p. 35.
4. Ibid., p. 2.
5. G. Paul Musselman, "Evangelism and the Disinherited," from *Evangelism and Contemporary Issues*, edited by Gordon Pratt Baker (Nashville: Tidings Press, 1964), p. 100.
6. Georgia Harkness, "Evangelism and Secularism," from *Evangelism and Contemporary Issues*, op. cit., p. 71.
7. Bryan Green, *The Practice of Evangelism* (New York: Charles Scribner's Sons, 1951), p. 16.
8. W. E. Sangster, *Let Me Commend* (Nashville: Abingdon Press, 1948), p. 14.
9. S. Paul Schilling, "The Meaning of Evangelism," from *Evangelism and Contemporary Issues*, op. cit., p. 9.

10. Douglas Webster, *What is Evangelism?* (London: The Highway Press, 1964), p. 105.
11. Robert Beach Cunningham, "Evangelism and the Challenge of the City," from *Evangelism and Contemporary Issues*, op. cit., p. 94.
12. Faris Daniel Whitesell, *Basic New Testament Evangelism* (Grand Rapids: Zondervan, 1949), p. 133.
13. Leighton Ford, *The Christian Persuader* (New York: Harper and Row, 1966), p. 45.
14. *The Church for Others* (Geneva: World Council of Churches, 1968), pp. 18-19.
15. C. E. Autrey, *Basic Evangelism* (Grand Rapids: Zondervan, 1954), p. 63.
16. Joseph Henry Thayer, *A Greek-English Lexicon of the New Testament* (New York: American Book Company, 1886), p. 536. H. J. Carpenter in *A Theological Wordbook of the Bible* holds that only some in the body of elders in a church would have the function of *episkopoi* (p. 150).
17. Ibid., p. 137.
18. William Barclay, *The Letters to the Galatians and Ephesians in the Daily Study Bible Series* (Philadelphia: Westminster Press, 1956), pp. 171 ff.
19. Ibid., p. 175.
20. Faris Daniel Whitesell, op. cit., p. 144.
21. C. E. Autrey, op. cit., p. 66.

35-39
50-58
38-54
139-158

2 A Theology of Evangelism

If the church would effectively evangelize today, it must do so from a strong theological base. It has been quite correctly stated that "there can be no effective and permanent evangelism without theology, and there would soon be few persons ready to study theology without evangelism." [1] If evangelism loses sight of theology, it does so at its own peril. And theology divorced from the fervor of evangelism is dry and tasteless. It cannot be stated too strongly that the two disciplines, when separated, part to their mutual detriment.

Reasons for Uniting Theology and Evangelism

There are very sound reasons why theology and mission must not be separated. The first and by far the most important reason is that they are never divorced in the Scriptures. This is evident by the simple fact that the books of the New Testament were not composed primarily as dissertations on Christian theology; rather, they were the "incidental literature of evangelism." [2] It is clear, for example, that many of Paul's most profound doctrinal statements grew out of an evangelistic and pastoral concern for the churches. At the same time they give us in unsystematic form the very essence of our Christian theology. This stands to reason, for evangelism by its very name implies a theology. It is the good news that God has revealed about himself. Thus it can be put in propositional form. It can be discussed. Its implications can be formulated. And this is theology. So the evangelistic passion grows out of doctrinal sources. From the purely biblical perspective, the two go hand in glove.

A second reason for the wedding of theology and mission is that without sound theological content, evangelism soon degenerates into sentimentalism, emotionalism, and gimmicks. Such charges have at times been directed towards the evangelistically minded. Sadly enough, all too often there is substance to the criticisms. And it is rather dishonest—and may even betray a simple laziness—for the evangelical to retort that such a charge grows out of spiritual coldness and a lack of concern for the unbelieving world. Any form of evangelism that resorts to the manipulation of people, regardless of the motive, is unworthy of the gospel. Even more tragically, such an experience can lead unsuspecting and honest inquirers into a shallow experience that falls short of a genuine experience of salvation. Scriptural evangelism demands that the evangelist fill his presentation of the gospel with solid theological content. It is a price that must be paid if God's approval on the work is expected, for people are rarely if ever genuinely converted by psychological maneuvering, persuasive oratory, or emotional stories devoid of the impact of the Holy Spirit. For the sake of those whom we would reach for Christ, authentic theology and evangelism must not be severed.

The third reason for fusing theology and evangelism is the pragmatic fact that God has honored most profoundly the ministry of those who do. A mere cursory survey of the history of mission clearly demonstrates this principle. The early church fathers are a patent instance. Augustine of Hippo in the fourth and fifth centuries was a great theologian. His system of thought was foundational in his own day, but it also had significant influence on the reformers a millennium later. Yet he was also a very effective evangelist. His great work *The City of God* was inspired directly by the spirit of mission. Concerning Christian theology, Augustine said it "must be carried into practice, and . . . taught for the very purpose of being practiced . . . ; the preacher must sway the mind so as to subdue the will." He demonstrated in his ministry that beautiful blend of theology and evangelism. Illustrations of this type can be multiplied over and again in the lives of men like Calvin, Luther, Arminius, Wesley, and Whitefield. In more recent times the principle is seen in evangelists like Charles Finney, the great American preacher of the nineteenth century whose ministry won thousands while he was also teaching theology at Oberlin College for over forty years. R. A. Torrey, a very successful evangelist, was a highly competent student; he read his polyglot Bible every day. And a number of our own contemporaries could be stated.

One can conclude from a purely practical perspective that God uses most significantly the man who blends with his evangelistic ministry a sound theology. C. E. Autry declared: "Theology is to evangelism what the skeleton is to the body. Remove the skeleton and the body becomes a helpless quivering mass of jelly-like substance. By means of the skeleton the body can stand erect and move. The great systems of theological truths form the skeleton which enables our revealed religion to stand." [3]

Other reasons could be given for the necessity of a strong theology for effective evangelism. For example, a knowledge of theology makes the presentation of the gospel message plain; it makes the evangelist more sure of his message; a genuine understanding of the rich content of the Bible will fill one with zeal; theology is an important agent in conserving evangelistic results. But the major reasons given above should convince any Christian who seeks to win the unbeliever that theology and mission must be forever united.

Therefore, the pastor-evangelist must formulate a strong theology of evangelism. Space will obviously preclude any attempt to present a thorough-going doctrinal statement of mission. It may even appear a bit presumptuous to give only one chapter to a theme that can boast volumes. Yet there are basic truths one must make ingredient to his life of outreach if he is to be effective in mission activity. So we shall be brave and briefly discuss these aspects of theology to present at least a working outline for the pastor-evangelist.

The Necessity of Conversion

It seems obvious that the biblical presentation of the necessity of conversion is the first foundation stone in building a theology of evangelism. It may appear to some as quite unnecessary even to approach such a well-known doctrine. Yet today this truth is implicitly, if not explicitly, being more and more called into question. The growing spirit of syncretism and universalism is being felt even in circles that have been traditionally evangelical and evangelistic. This is especially true among younger educated people.

The necessity of conversion clearly rests on the scriptural doctrine of man and his sin. As has often been said, to understand the good news of God we must first understand the bad news of man.[4] Appropriately, therefore, in the early chapters of Genesis we have the account of the creation of man, his corruption by sin, and the consequences of his willful disobedience. The Bible thereafter uses several figures to describe man in his rebellious state. He is seen as corrupted, blind, diseased, lost, dead, etc. These ideas are all efforts to portray the fact that something is terribly awry with human character. The Bible sees man's very nature and personhood as severely perverted from his true humanity. There is absolutely no scriptural warrant for holding the view that man is essentially good, even despite the fact that he was created in God's image (Rom. 7:18). Man stands in desperate need. He is in real trouble. But where is this trouble rooted? Rutenber has correctly said it lies in an utter "failure of relationships."[5]

Man is never a mere object. He is not an atomic simple. He is not "just there." Man can never be understood apart from his basic relationships. These essential relationships, Rutenber tells us, are three; his relation to God, his relation to his fellows, and his relation to himself. He is related to God in that he is made for fellowship with God. This is the meaning of the "image of God." He is made in and for the love of God. This makes him responsible and human. Secondly, he is related to his fellows in a social sense. No man can be "an island entire to itself alone." Inter-human relationships are a vital part of that which makes life what it is. Finally, man is related to himself, i.e. he can talk to himself, he can think about himself; in a word, he has self-consciousness. Moreover, he can have a hand in the forging of his own character and personality.

Sin Corrupts Life's Relationships

When man becomes disobedient to God, all of his basic relationships are corrupted. Sin bludgeons every important tie that makes life worth living. To begin with, sin in the divine-human relationship results in a deep sense of guilt. And it is genuine guilt, not just neurotic guilt feelings. Sin is a refusal by man to let God act in his life, i.e. to be God in a real sense. This makes one truly guilty before God. Naturally guilt feelings arise. They should—man *is* guilty. He is culpable. He stands condemned. Judgment—eternal judgment—is his lot, for the essential God-man relationship is corrupted.

In the second place, sin in relation to one's fellows precipitates a spirit of lovelessness. The only thing that holds the structures of society together in harmony is love. When love degenerates, society with its vital human relationships also crumbles. Little wonder that the world is in the condition it is! With love gone, only selfishness remains—even if it is very cultured or restrained by law. Lastly, sin in relation to one's own self means bondage, perversion, frustration, and depression. Self-relatedness is corrupted by evil just as surely as are the other essential relationships of life. One can only "be himself" when properly related to God and others. As Rutenber graphically describes it: "With God lost, I am thrown back on myself to live off my own nerves and feed off my own fingernails." [6] Thus, sin perverts all of life; man is guilty, loveless, and in bondage.

Though sin and rebellion mean more, perhaps much more, it should at least be clear that man stands in desperate need of change. And a little straightening up here and there will never do. He stands in need of radical, revolutionary change. He needs to become a whole new man. His entire system of relationships cries out to be healed. He needs reconciliation at a profound level. He needs to die and start over again. And that is just what conversion means. It is the "turn" that utterly transforms life. That is why we contend vigorously for the absolute necessity of conversion.

Now the fact of man's need is the rationale behind the scriptural call to repentance and faith, for this alone brings about a true conversion experience. The Bible is unmistakably clear in its demands for such an in-depth exercise of the will. As Michael Green, in his excellent work *Evangelism in the Early Church*, has said;

> . . . although it [salvation] is absolutely universal in its offer, Mark knows that the good news is only effective among those who repent, believe, and are prepared to engage in costly, self-sacrificial discipleship. Only the man who is prepared to lose his life for the sake of Christ and the gospel can find it; for it was only in losing his life for the sake of others that Christ could offer a new life to men, the new life proclaimed in the gospel.[7]

In the light of these truths it seems strange that some seemingly desire to downgrade the inescapable necessity of a conversion experience for all peoples. Perhaps it grows out of a misunderstanding of the nature or message of the Bible or a shallow grasp of the real condition of man. I do not suppose many will be very zealous in their evangelistic labors until they are utterly convinced of these facts and experience the compassion of Christ concerning the depth of man's plight. These truths are surely vital to a dynamic theology of evangelism.

God as Redeemer

This leads us to investigate what God has done to remedy man's awful sickness. As we have seen, the Scriptures paint a dark and somber picture of man's sin. But they also paint a bright portrait of God as the Redeemer and Reconciler of man. The whole Bible is saying in clear and forceful fashion: God redeems.

God redeems as Father. He desires men to become his sons, so he sent his Son. He reveals himself as Father, for he desires that we live in that relationship. He is King, and he wishes man to submit to that authority. He is the giver of life, desiring all to receive its fullness. Above all, he is love, and so he pleads with us to receive that love and walk in a fellowship of love with him.

God redeems as Son. This is obvious; the "good news" is the news about the Son. The entire Christ-event is all about redemption. This is the essence of the incarnation. It was what Jesus Christ did as man that made it possible for him to do anything for man. The cross is all redemption, from the first blow of the hammer in piercing his hand until the cry, "It is finished." "In my place condemned He stood. Sealed my pardon with His blood. Hallelujah! What a Saviour." Further, the resurrection means a redeemed life. The Christian experience is a perpetual Easter. Little wonder Paul wrote, "We preach Christ."

God redeems as Holy Spirit. It is he who convinces of sin, righteousness, and judgment (John 16:7-11). It is he who inspires faith. It is he who is the agent in the regeneration experience (John 3:5,8). It is he who seals the newborn Christian (Eph. 1:3). It is he who comes to abide as God in the human life and thus makes the human body the temple of God (1 Cor. 6:19). It is he who transforms the believer into a truly different person by "forming Christ within" (Gal. 4:19). Apart from the working of the Holy Spirit, there is no personal redemption. The Holy Spirit makes the saving Christ one's constant contemporary. Therefore, we conclude that all three persons of the triune Godhead are involved in man's reconciliation.

The Necessity of Confidence in the Atonement of Christ

Concerning the atonement that God has accomplished in Christ we must give more detailed attention. Grasping the meaning of the atonement is essential to a sound theology of mission; for from this develops that confidence in the reconciling work of Jesus Christ that will motivate one to proclaim fearlessly and joyously its tremendous truths.

There was a time when much interest was shown in the various theories of the atonement. Theologians would elucidate in some detail each concept and then discuss at length its various merits and defects. Space, if not contemporary interest, forbids such a detailed exercise here. It may still be helpful to see at least the salient contribution the different theories have given to our understanding of the work of Christ. It is somewhat difficult to classify the various ideas of atonement, but the following may suffice.

Theories of the Atonement

The governmental (Grotian) theory. This concept of the atonement, recently defended by A. B. Crabtree, tells us that Christ was essentially a substitute for us. He stood in our place and bore our penalty. It views the atonement as a satisfaction but not as an internal principle of the divine nature. This is its obvious weakness. Yet the law and its demands had to be met, and Christ accomplished this when he died in our place and bore our judgment in himself. Here is one aspect of the truth to be fully understood and forthrightly proclaimed in the presentation of the gospel. We are pardoned because Christ bore our punishment.

The example (Socinian) theory. This approach to atonement states that by Christ's example man is motivated to reconcile himself to God. The weakness of this approach, as its very name implies, rests in its failure to grasp the fact that God must also be seen as reconciled to man in the work of Christ as well as the converse. Vincent has apparently grasped this truth when he speaks of God's "transformed face" towards sinners. But at least the theory does point out, and quite correctly, that man desperately needs reconciling to God, i.e. that the basic divine-human relationship must be restored. It has further seen that the death of Christ is a beautiful example of faithfulness to truth and duty and, thus, has a powerful influence on one's own moral improvement. Christ's example of love and sacrifice should kindle a similar love in us. Of course, the cross is far more than example, yet it surely is that also. The so-called Bushnellian or moral influence theory has much the same approach with its attendant failings and strong points.

The commercial (Anselmic) theory. The impact of this conception of the atoning work of Christ rests in its grasp of the fact that the divine honor is grossly sinned against in man's rebellion. The consequences are that eternal punishment must attend the offender. But it suffers from a lack of understanding that more than the divine honor is at stake in man's sin. Moreover, the atonement at Calvary did far more than meet the divine claims in an exact equivalent, as this theory implies. The work of Christ on the cross was not that formal and external. And the divine honor cannot become more prominent than divine holiness. Still one must grant that God's honor was involved in it all and in that sense the concept has something to say.

The dramatic (patristic) theory. Here the emphasis is on the struggle between the forces of God and the forces of evil. In one sense this tends to leave man somewhat out of the picture in its stress on the struggle of opposing forces. Surely man was deeply involved in the whole affair. At the same time, however, it is clear that a great battle was being waged and the forces of evil were routed and destroyed in the Christ-event.

The ransom theory. This is also sometimes called the patristic view. Further, it is something of a variation of the above concept. The idea is that if we were redeemed through a ransom paid by God, the one who was paid must have been Satan. Few hold such a morally repugnant view today; although Aulen, in his *Christus Victor,* proposes something of a demythologized view of the concept. True, our salvation was very costly to God, but he hardly paid a ransom for captive men to the devil or anyone. The truth to be stressed in the concept of a ransom paid is that the atonement price was the costly blood of Christ, and God who paid that price is thus the great deliverer. We shall expand this in more detail when later in this chapter we consider the idea of justification.

The ethical theory. A. H. Strong attempts to bring together the strengths of these other views in the approach he conceived and called the ethical theory. He makes the following points: (a) the atonement must be seen as rooted in the holiness of God; (b) it must answer the ethical demands of the divine nature; (c) in the humanity of Christ and his sufferings all claims of justice are met; (d) Christ suffered vicariously; (e) the atonement was accomplished through the solidarity of the race; (f) it satisfies man's ethical needs; (g) the atonement is for all, but man must avail himself of it.

Whether or not we agree with all Strong asks for, it seems he has grasped the importance of gleaning from the various theories those aspects of truth they present and then incorporating them into a full system. This approach has obvious value, for the atonement is a many-faceted jewel. To fix one's gaze upon just one facet is to neglect the beauty of the whole. So profound is the scriptural presentation of the atonement that a completely satisfying theology is most difficult, if not impossible. The more we look into its wonders, the more glorious it becomes. But we must continue our gaze and continue to pass on to others what wonders we discover.

There are other, modern, quite unique interpretations of the atonement. These are of great interest but must be left for more critical studies. Now perhaps a brief excursion into some of the various biblical words that describe salvation will help us most in gaining deeper understanding and more profound confidence in the atonement of Christ.

The Biblical Meaning of Salvation

A term we have already used several times is *conversion.* The New Testament word-group is based on the Greek word *epis-*

trephein. As could be expected, this group is used in classical and koine Greek in a non-theological sense. It means simply "to turn" as to turn a ship or to turn oneself around. It can also connote "to turn the mind" or "turn one's attention to." Etymologically this led to the usage; "to warn," "to correct," "to cause to repent." Thus, we see it acquiring religious overtones. Quite naturally, therefore, the New Testament writers picked it up. It was ideally suited to present the concept behind conversion. In the Scriptures themselves, the word-group in its substantial and verbal forms is used some thirty-five times. It is rarely used in a transitive sense except in Luke 1:17 and James 5:19-20. It is frequently used in a physical sense of turning or returning, e.g. Matthew 12:44, Luke 2:39. But for our immediate interest, it is most often employed to connote a mental or spiritual turn. Classic examples are Peter's call to repentance in Acts 3:19 and the account of Acts 9:35 where many "turned" to the Lord. The Old Testament equivalent *shubh* occurs some 1,146 times and is used in much the same fashion as the *epistrephein* word-group. The basic theological idea is this: one is called to turn, to change the direction of his thinking, affections, willing, etc. It implies a complete reversal of all of life. This indicates that he turns *from* something *to* something. He turns from himself to God. As Brunner has expressed it, repentance is coming alive to one's true self as a sinner and faith is coming to God as a Savior. This is conversion.

Redemption is a very common word in current theological writings. This wide use of the term is a relatively modern development. It is not used abundantly in the New Testament, and theologians normally followed that pattern until quite recent times. When the word was employed by older writers, it was used in a much more restricted sense. The man in the street of the first century thought of it in a completely non-religious sense—as is the case with so many of the terms that now have deep theological implications. The basic word is *lutron*, i.e. ransom. The term is derived from *luō*, meaning to loose. It was used to describe almost any kind of loosing, like the loosing of men from prison. However, in such a case, when one was loosed as a prisoner of war a ransom price was paid. Hence the concept of release on receipt of ransom grew up around the term. As Morris points out, "this idea of payment as the basis of release . . . is the reason for the existence of the whole word-group." [8] The Hebrew equivalents are: *g'l* where only Yahweh is used as the subject of the verbal forms; *pah* where the idea is of a ransom acquired by the payment of a price; and *kopher* which means the actual ransom price itself.

So we can see that the basic biblical concept of redemption is the paying of a ransom price to secure a liberation. When God is the subject of the verb, there is a shift of emphasis. It is not conceivable, as Morris correctly states, that God could pay a ransom to man, and surely not to the devil as the old ransom theory of the atonement holds. The stress must be placed upon the idea of deliverance rather than on the means by which it is brought about. At the same time, however, the thought is there that God delivers his people at a cost—and at a high cost. We know of course what that cost was: the precious blood of Christ (1 Pet. 1:18-19). Consequently, "Believers are not brought by Christ into a liberty of selfish ease. Rather since they have been bought by God at terrible cost, they have become God's slaves, to do His will." [9] A proper understanding and declaration of this tremendous truth should save us from a shallow evangelism.

It would appear that the dominating idea in Paul's concept of salvation is found in the word *justification*. This is true if one can judge from the sheer number of times he employs the thought. The word-group from which this term derives is *dikaios*, i.e. "righteous." The basic idea is a "proper standing before God." It is a status of righteousness conferred on men by God upon the basis of the work of Christ in his death and resurrection. Emphasis must be laid on the idea of imputation, for there is no sense in which such a status can be attained by human works of righteousness. The roots of the doctrine are found in the Old Testament view of righteousness, and Morris contends it is vital to realize this to appreciate the New Testament meaning of salvation. God in his holiness demands righteousness among men. This the law clearly demonstrates. Many first-century Jews seemingly saw this as performing deeds of legal righteousness. The New Testament, however, presents it as an imputed righteousness. For man is a sinner and cannot be righteous in himself. But Christ died for all and fulfilled the demands of the law in our stead. Classical Protestantism has always interpreted the idea to mean that Christ endured the penalty of sin and in this way demonstrated that the eternal law of righteousness cannot be disputed. As Calvin put it, "As the law allowed no remission, and God did remit sins, there appeared to be a stain on divine justice. The exhibition of Christ as an atonement is what alone removes it." [10]

So a man is justified, made righteous in God's sight, when he exercises faith in the atoning work of Christ. Faith opens up to him this new status. The forensic implications of the concept are clear, and our communicating of the gospel should make them plain. Lenski holds that *dikaios* is always forensic.

It may well be that the most relevant aspect of salvation to our day centers in the truths implied by the word *reconciliation.* We have already pointed out in some detail that man lives in a threefold relationship, i.e. to God, his fellows, and himself. It is the rupturing of these vital relationships that comprises the tragedy of sin. Man in rebellion toward God is guilty, loveless, and under bondage. Reconciliation means the restoring of these essential and vital relationships.

Rutenber interestingly points out that modern psychiatry is deeply involved with these three problems in man. But it is clear that the psychiatrist deals with them on an entirely different level than the Christian witness. The problems of guilt, inability to give and/or receive love, and lack of freedom to function properly in society occupies the counselor constantly. But though the psychiatrist may remove neurotic guilt, real guilt remains; and though he may enable a loveless neurotic to give and receive love on a human level, only Christ can impart by his Holy Spirit the *agape* love of God; and though the doctor may help a man find release from fear so as to function more successfully as a useful member of society, only the new birth gives one the true liberty of the sons of God. In other words, "psychiatry and the gospel work on a man's problems on different though not unrelated levels. The well-integrated, well-adjusted, and socially well-manicured person still needs redemption." [11]

It is this preoccupation of the contemporary psychiatrist with these problems that demonstrates the need of man for reconciliation. And Christ's salvation provides it in true depth. First, one is reconciled to God, for salvation means forgiveness—real forgiveness for real sin. God freely pardons us in Christ. This forgiveness clearly reaches much deeper than just neurotic guilt feelings. True guilt before God and its attending feelings are eradicated. One can say with Paul, "We have peace with God through our Lord Jesus Christ" (Rom. 5:1, KJV). Moreover, through Christ's work in death and resurrection, God is genuinely reconciled to man. This is a theological truth not to be overlooked. Reconciliation is a two-way street. God has been offended and needs reconciliation towards man. That too is accomplished in the Christ-event. Consequently, the sinner recognizes God's moral prerogative to forgive *justly* in Christ. For before forgiveness becomes morally effective, the conscience and moral sense of the forgiven must be satisfied. And Christ completely meets these demands, and Christian reconciliation with its marvelous peace is met on this double level of depth. The forgiven sinner knows God has not "leaned over backwards" to forgive him. God remains just and yet the justifier of those who believe (Rom. 3:26). Forgiveness and reconciliation can be offered on a basis that the forgiven one is not humiliated and his self-respect taken away. Moreover, the moral structure of the universe is safeguarded. As Rutenber has reminded us, "The cross makes forgiveness possible without making righteousness secondary." [12]

Reconciled to God, man is now free to love his fellows, be reconciled to them, and become a reconciling agent. But even the man in Christ cannot love as he should if he relies solely on his humanity. So God sheds his *agape* love abroad in our hearts by the Holy Spirit (Rom. 5:5). In a very real sense, Christ loves through us. The quality of this love is obviously much different from the *eros* love of the world, as Nygren has told us. [13] This *agape* kind of love is an interested love; it demonstrates an infinitely imaginative interest in the well-being of others. It is persistent, continually persistent, in meeting needs. Further, it is not given because the object of love is loveable or fills a vacuum in the life of the lover; that is love on the *eros* level. Rather, it is unconditional; there are no "ifs" or "buts" about it. It loves regardless of the response, the character of the one loved, or the reaction of society. And it is nonsentimental, nonindulgent, mature. It always seeks the best for the other even though it may be quite painful. *Agape* is always vulnerable, open to suffering. In a word, *agape* love is reconciling. It takes the initiative and heals, restores, and cures broken lives and relationships because it is completely selfless. This is God's kind of love and the kind of love demonstrated to us in Christ. And with Christ in one's life, this reconciling love is bestowed on others. If these truths are not relevant to today's ruptured society, one wonders what is.

Finally, reconciled to God and one's fellows, man is also reconciled to himself and is free—really free—to function as a mature member of society. We tend to think of our sophisticated culture with its rejection of the old superstitions, taboos, and animism of the past as one quite free from fear. That which formerly bound the human personality has now been shown up as false, we are told. Man is thus free from the shackles of fear. We can grow and expand. I wonder! True, we have laid to rest much which should have been buried long ago. But is not our problem that of a basic inner bondage?

Though our cultural development and enlightenment has eliminated the old outward manifestations of that bondage, I doubt it has done a great deal to solve the real difficulty—man's estrangement from his true self. Instead of laying our fears to the influence of some evil spirit in a tree as man once did, we now attribute it to some negative experience of childhood or fear of the bomb. This may be a better diagnosis of the sickness, but what we need is a cure. Man is still in bondage to himself. As Paul put it in Romans, "I do not understand my own actions. For I do not do what I want, but I do the very thing I hate. . . . I see in my members another law at war with the law of my mind and making me captive" (Rom. 7:15, 23).

But in Christ one is truly free. He is freed from that imprisonment to his corrupt self; he is free from the fear of the future and the past; his fear of men dissipates; the enslavement of guilt goes; and he can really breathe deeply for the first time. Life takes on meaning. The questions of today's youth: who am I? and where am I going? are satisfyingly answered. He does not have to stand on the corner with Beckett and wait for Godot to come—Godot comes. He truly becomes an "authentic self." That is reconciliation, and that is most applicable to today's bewildered, meaningless world. So man stands in the salvation the Godhead provides. Because God is concerned with the whole man, the needs of the whole man are met in the Lord Jesus Christ.

There are other biblical concepts concerning salvation that space simply forbids our considering, e.g. propitiation, adoption, new creation, covenant, and so on. But perhaps the bare outline of these aspects of redemption may enable us to begin developing such utter and complete confidence in the atonement of Jesus Christ that we shall herald that good news with a positive joy and enthusiasm.

Confidence in the Power of the Gospel

This ushers us into a brief consideration of the importance of acquiring confidence in the actual message we are to proclaim.

Paul said, "I am not ashamed of the gospel: it is the power of God for salvation to everyone who has faith" (Rom. 1:16, RSV). Such must be our spirit and attitude. The right approach was voiced by C. H. Spurgeon when on a certain occasion a young ministerial student asked him how to defend successfully the gospel. Spurgeon replied, "How do you defend a lion? You don't, you just turn him loose." But is one justified in having such confidence in the gospel? The answer is yes, because it is the good news about God from God. Its source and its content are divine. This is why confidence in the power of the message can be seen as most reasonable to the Christian.

This clearly implies that we need not—yea, must not—rely on human ingenuity alone, psychological manipulations, dramatics, or any mere human invention to convince men of the truth and relevance of the message. God will speak for himself through his Word. His Holy Spirit will press home the truth. The gospel truly is "the power of God unto salvation."

Furthermore, the gospel speaks directly to the human situation as no other truth. Whether or not man will admit his desperate need of reconciliation, that is his actual and deepest longing. The gospel always stands as the most relevant message he can hear. This point we have been laboring. But it is right here that we must be most careful. We must present the gospel to the living human situation. We must never simply grind out the truth—even gospel truth—in a barrage of clichés. A cold delivery of evangelical orthodoxy is fatal. Just "delivering a message" can be in one sense a "savor of death unto death" (2 Cor. 2:16, KJV). We speak to real people in real human situations. Their sin is real and concrete. Their fears, frustrations, and thwarted ambitions have genuine substance. They are involved in a true social context. They cry for help where they are. What I am trying to say is, it is people that matter. People matter as much as principle. Our Lord's ministry reflected this. He addressed men in their actual living situation. He talked about concrete, contemporary issues. He never compromised principle, but it was always addressed in love to people in their personal, immediate needs.

Many who are evangelistically minded need to be reminded of this. Some seem so concerned with orthodoxy they forget that truth standing alone is irrelevant—if not an outright abstraction. Orthodoxy is important, but it is the orthodox gospel put in the terms of life itself and presented in love to real people that God honors. But more of this later when we take up the problems of communication in today's complex world. Suffice it to say in summary that our message is one of power and relevance. It meets the deepest of human needs and we must have utter confidence in it if we are to be effective as the evangelistic church.

We are Co-Laborers with God

The fourth essential principle in a developing theology of evangelism is that expressed by Paul to the Corinthian believers: "We are God's fellow workers" (1 Cor. 3:9, RSV, margin). The rationale for this principle is found in the truth expressed in chapter 1 that the mission to evangelize is essentially God's mission, the *missio Dei*. As the working group of the World Council of Churches has stated, "Mission is basically understood as God working out His purpose for His creation; the church does not have a separate mission of its own. It is called to participate in God's mission. The missionary call is a call for participation." [14]

In a word, God is the Evangelist and we are merely laborers together with him. It is essentially God who does the work. This must be kept constantly before the church. We can so easily get bogged down in the details of either our biblical and theological studies or the practical work of the church that we miss this one central theme of the Scriptures. This is a truth we must never lose sight of. It will save us from a "sanctified humanism" that has so often plagued evangelism.

But as discussed earlier, there is a parallel truth—perhaps a paradoxical truth—that God never redeems anyone apart from the instrumentality of his people, the church. This may seem an overstatement, yet the Scriptures bear it out. Pentecost's thousands came to Christ through the witness of Peter and the Twelve. Cornelius, though addressed by an angel, heard the gospel itself from Simon. Paul, who was actually accosted by the glorified Christ himself, heard what he was to do from Ananias. And though sent by an angel, it was still Philip who taught the Ethiopian eunuch about Christ. Through the New Testament and subsequent church history the principle persists. In commenting on this truth, Lenski points out, "Here we see how Jesus honors His ministry. Philip is sent to the eunuch by an angel; it is not the angel who is sent to teach the eunuch. And this is the case wherever the gospel is to be offered." [15]

These principles involve two important implications relative to the church. First, we can be assured of success because God is with us—or perhaps we should say that we are with God. Of course, success cannot be judged by human standards. But if this is God's work in which we are engaged as co-laborers, final success is certain. This should be a great encouragement and a strong stimulus to tireless effort. We are never alone.

Secondly, an awesome responsibility is put on the church. If God has no other plan for world redemption outside of the use of the agency of his people, the mandate to cooperate with God in his work is pressing indeed. Therefore, it is essential to the kingdom that we enthusiastically engage in this work. A short time ago I was preaching along the line of the necessity of Christians becoming witnesses for Christ. Perhaps I was waxing a bit too eloquent, but I made the statement that unless God's people become enthusiastic witnesses, many will not be converted. After the service a young lady challenged me on my statement. She contended that those whom God has elected will be converted regardless of what we do. I suppose there is an element of truth on that side of the paradoxical coin of election and freedom. But there is also the other side which declares that God uses his people in his quest for men, and the implications of what will happen if God's people fail in the mission can be legitimately drawn. At least Ezekiel seemed to think so. He tells us:

> So you, son of man, I have made a watchman for the house of Israel; whenever you hear a word from my mouth, you shall give them warning from me. If I say to the wicked, O wicked man, you shall surely die, and you do not speak to warn the wicked to turn from his way, that wicked man shall die in his iniquity, but his blood I shall require at your hand. But if you warn the wicked to turn from his way, and he does not turn from his way, he shall die in his iniquity, but you will have saved your life. (Ezek. 33:7-8, RSV)

My interview with the young lady was somewhat reminiscent of William Carey's encounter with the old brother who told him to sit down after his plea for missionaries, for if God wanted to convert the heathen he would do it without Carey's help. We are thankful today that Carey did not sit down but zealously went after men for Christ. Such must be the attitude of the contemporary church if we take seriously the principle of being co-laborers with God. This to me seems vital for a sound theology of evangelism. The local church as a whole must be motivated to engage in mission and I do not believe it will get involved unless it gets rooted in a sound understanding of the *missio Dei.*

Finally, in exploring a theology of evangelism, let us look briefly at

The Basic Biblical Principles of Evangelistic Methodology

This theme could become a volume in itself. It is therefore quite difficult to attempt to deal with it in a few words. Yet it is vital to see, if only in simplest form, some of these important principles, because evangelistic activity that neglects or ignores biblical methodologies is doomed to failure. Tersely put, we must do God's work in God's way. Let us look first briefly into the ministry of our Lord and then at the early church.

Note ten salient points from the ministry of Christ.

1. Primarily, Jesus unreservedly gave of himself; he shared his own personhood on behalf of the needy. He did this in a fashion we never can; yet we must emulate the principle if we are to be effective as evangelists. This is foundational.

2. He confronted people with the great issues. He was never sidetracked on theological fads. He kept on the main line. Yet he dealt with these great, profound truths with a marvellous simplicity. "The common people heard him gladly" (Mark 12:37, KJV). The preacher who overshoots his people is not following Jesus' example.

3. He never compromised the demanding claims of the gospel to win followers. He always presented his absolute lordship as the cost of discipleship. He never cut corners to gain anyone; the classic case was that of the rich young ruler.

4. At the same time, he had profound respect for human personality. He never bulldozed anyone. He was always patient, understanding, and loving. He was characterized by dignity—and that in a good, mature sense. He never made anyone less of a person even in his occasional scathing denunciations.

5. He presented the truth uncompromisingly and challenged men to decide then and there. He asked Simon and Andrew, James and John to choose right then between their nets or discipleship (Mark 1:16-20). Matthew was directly and pointedly confronted with the life-deciding issue of whether it would be God or mammon. And he had to decide while he sat right at the tax-collector's bench that was loaded with mammon. There is a principle implied here that many need to grasp today. So often we just leave the gospel for people "to think over" in such a nebulous way that we rob it of its challenge to immediate commitment. There is the time to wait, to be sure, but there is also the time to call men to decision.

6. It seems evident from the life of our Lord that he had a definite strategy. For example, "His face was set towards Jerusalem" (Luke 9:53). Jesus knew what he was about and where he was going. To

update this principle into modern terms, he had a program. This, too, we desperately need to learn. We shall be considering this principle later.

7. He did not attempt to do all the work himself. He taught, encouraged, nurtured, and commissioned his disciples. The implications of this fact are clear and numerous as regards the local church.

8. He was above all compassionate. He saw the people as sheep without a shepherd. No personal sacrifice was ever too great to hinder our Lord from ministering. He was always in the spirit of the towel and basin washing feet. For he said, "The Son of man came not to be served but to serve, and to give his life" (Matt. 20:28).

9. He ministered to the whole man. Physical, mental, and spiritual needs were met quite indiscriminately by Jesus. Whatever or wherever needs arose, he met them. He knew little of the so-called divisions of secular and sacred, spiritual and physical, or saving and social gospel.

10. Lastly, he saw prayer as the one indispensable exercise in his mission. How can it be otherwise with us? Thus our Lord ministered his good news and people came by the multitudes to see and hear—and not a few believed.

Let us take a final look at Pentecost as something of a model for local church evangelism. Granted, much more than evangelistic principles is implied by the day of Pentecost; that day was a great epoch in the church. Still there is much that can be learned concerning local mission by the events of the day, that is, provided we attempt to do so without doing violence to the other great theological truths of Pentecost and provided we recognize that many of these truths are the most prominent in the scriptural account.

First of all, it is evident that Pentecost is telling us that this is the age of the Spirit. God has not withdrawn from salvation history with the ascension of Jesus Christ. Just the converse is true; he is now in the work as profoundly as in the days of his flesh. All effective mission is carried on in the context of a Spirit-led, inspired, and energized ministry.

Pentecost also points up the fact that before anything happens significantly in the unbelieving community, something of great significance must happen to the church. The city of Jerusalem took little note of the 120 followers of the Nazarene gathered for ten days. But when the disciples were deeply moved upon by God, "the multitude came together." And they were "confounded," "amazed," "perplexed" until they finally just gave up trying to discover a rationale for the phenomenon and asked, "What does this mean?" It was then—and not until then—that Peter could stand up and say, "This is that!" and present Christ. This is always ideally the context of great evangelism. The outside world becomes so perplexed by the wonder of what God has done and is doing in and through his church that they begin asking questions. It is in this kind of setting that the gospel can be most effectively communicated. Surely all of us earnestly pray for such a move of God's Spirit upon his church.

Of prime importance, on the day of Pentecost, Christ was preached. The disciples had but one message. This does not mean that later we do not see the New Testament church ministering in many different ways and preaching many different truths. They were not afraid of the social implications of the gospel, for example. It surely does not mean they did not confront men in their own life situation and approach them with that particular aspect of the good news that was most appealing and relevant. But whether we see Stephen addressing the biblical-oriented Sanhedrin, Peter appealing to the God-fearing Gentile Cornelius, or Paul preaching to the philosophical sophisticates of Athens, they approached these different people with their different references of thought and simply presented Christ as the answer to life's basic needs. Here is an inescapable principle for effective evangelistic endeavor and a vital part of a sound theology of mission.

It is recognized, as we bring this chapter to a close, that this mere skeleton of a theology of evangelism needs much meat hung on the bare bones. But if the Spirit can breathe upon us, it is hoped that these bones can live. With this framework of theology, therefore, let us move on to consider the more practical aspects and problems of evangelism.

Notes

1. C. E. Autrey, *Basic Evangelism*, op. cit., p. 13.
2. A. Skevington Wood, *Evangelism, Its Theology and Practice* (Grand Rapids: Zondervan, 1966), p. 11.
3. C. E. Autrey, op. cit., p. 16.
4. Culbert G. Rutenber, *The Reconciling Gospel* (Philadelphia: Judson Press, 1960), p. 41.
5. Ibid., p. 41.
6. Ibid., p. 46.
7. Michael Green, *Evangelism in the Early Church* (London: Hodder and Stoughton, 1970), pp. 53-4.
8. Leon Morris, *The Apostolic Preaching of the Cross* (London: Tyndale Press, 1955), p. 12.
9. Ibid., p. 54.
10. Ibid., p. 279.
11. Culbert G. Rutenber, op. cit., p. 48.
12. Ibid., p. 55.
13. The volume entitled *Agape and Eros* by Andres Nygren is a classic on this theme.
14. *The Church for Others*, p. 75.
15. R. H. C. Lenski, *The Interpretation of the Acts of the Apostles* (Minneapolis: Augsburg Publishing House, 1934), p. 355.

3 A Strategy of Outreach for Today

We have attempted to present the obligations of the pastor in developing an evangelistic church. But most pastors are quite knowledgeable of their responsibility to mission. Few have failed to grasp the implications of the Great Commission. One would further suppose that a large percentage have developed something of a theology of evangelism and are to a greater or lesser degree motivated to engage in the grand enterprise. The question that constantly comes up, however, is how can one evangelize today? At times there seems to be almost a spirit of frustration as evangelistically-minded Christians seek ways and means of implementing their theology of mission. This is understandable, especially in America and western Europe. We have never lived in a psychological and sociological atmosphere comparable to today's revolutionary spirit. And the old forms to which many congregations are shackled seemingly do not suffice to communicate the good news to the mass of contemporary men. What can be done? Is there an effective strategy for outreach that will work today? I believe we can answer this very basic query quite affirmatively. The solution is to be found in a principle as old as the Scriptures themselves. The key to effective mission in this or any generation rests essentially in the New Testament concept of the ministry of the laity.

The New Testament Principle of the Lay-centered Ministry

May I be bold and at the very outset state quite categorically that unless the church recaptures and implements the principle of a lay-centered ministry, I see little hope of fulfilling the commission to evangelize our day. It hardly seems necessary to present any kind of apologetic for the principle of a lay-centered ministry. Most pastors would be only too happy to see their lay people go to work. Moreover, most are aware, as Green tells us, that "Christianity was from its inception a lay movement, and so it continued for a remarkably long time." [1] Ministry for the early Christians was a happy, unselfconscious effort. They went about quite naturally sharing their faith, "gossiping the gospel" as it were. They were zealous, enthusiastic; they could not help but speak of the things they had experienced. They were not "professionals"; they were unpaid. As a consequence, they were taken seriously—especially was this true among the lower classes—and the movement spread like wildfire. As Green points out,

> All of this makes it abundantly clear that in contrast to the present day, when Christianity is highly intellectualized and dispensed by a professional clergy to a constituency increasingly confined to the middle classes, in the early days the faith was spontaneously spread by informal evangelists, and had its greatest appeal among the working classes.[2]

Simply put, through the ministry of these first-century laymen the masses were effectively reached with the gospel. It is reasonably conclusive that in the early church there was little if any distinction between full-time ministers and the laity, at least in the sense of responsibility to spread the good news. Every Christian was an evangelist. They well understood, as Goyder a layman himself has graphically put it, there are to be "no passengers in the church. All are called." [3]

It is regrettable that in these early years of church history clericalism began to develop. More and more, as the clergy assumed command of the evangelistic mission, the layman was slowly squeezed out. The clergy began to dominate the laity. Through the centuries this attitude hardened until in the course of time the English word "lay" became a synonym for "amateur" as over against "professional" or "unqualified" as opposed to "expert." How often we hear today, "I'm just a layman." This can usually be taken as an apology for not being able to do something very well. Of course some church members have not objected too vigorously to this development. More than a few have acquired a sort of "spectator mentality," and what the average member seems to want, as Sir John Lawrence states, is "a building which looks like a church; a clergyman dressed in a way he approves; services of the kind he's been used to, and to be left alone."[4] Such laymen have little if any real interest in evangelism, let alone actively engaging in the task.

On the other hand, there have been reactions to the clericalism of the contemporary church. Some have reacted very strongly, hence we have movements like the Quakers and Plymouth Brethren, who have virtually rejected the idea of a professional clergy all together. Other reactions have not been quite as cavalier but have nevertheless been very real. In the more traditional churches, for example, some laymen along with some ministers are asking if in today's world the clergy are really necessary. However, the bulk of Christians seemingly just accept some sort of dualism and acknowledge the need of ministers and laymen alike but have no real concept of the respective roles they play in the mission of the church. Yet a dualism of this sort is never satisfying and is a constant source of inefficiency if not irritation. Can such a situation find a resolution? It seems that it can in the biblical concept of the church as the body of Christ.

The Body Concept

There are many metaphors used in the New Testament to describe the people of God, the church. There are the figures of the church as the bride of Christ, God's vineyard, God's flock, the kingdom, the Father's family, God's building, a holy priesthood, the new Israel, and a holy nation. One of the most graphic, and that which seemed to be a favorite of Paul's, is to view the church as a body. This idea has two important implications relative to our consideration. First, as the human body has different parts with different functions, so the church. To say all members in a church are the same and are to do the same thing is rather ridiculous. Abilities and gifts vary with each member. "Are all apostles? Are all prophets? Are all teachers? Do all work miracles? Do all possess gifts of healing? Do all speak in tongues? Do all interpret? . . . For just as the body is one and has many members, and all the members of the body, though many, are one body, so it is with Christ. For by one Spirit we were all baptized into one body" (1 Cor. 12:29-30, 12-13). There is a diversity of members and corresponding functions in the local church that must be recognized.

The metaphor of the body also suggests that in the church's diversity there is also a central, inescapable unity. All the members stand equal and one before God. It is the one and same Spirit that enables all Christians to say, "Jesus is Lord." Moreover, as the body is a whole, so also is its basic task. The commission to evangelize is given to the entire body. John Stott reminds us that "the essential unity of the Church, originating in the call of God and illustrated in the metaphors of Scripture, leads us to this conclusion: the responsibilities which God has entrusted to His Church He has entrusted to His whole Church." [5] Now it is here that the dilemma of clericalism, anti-clericalism, and an unsatisfying dualism can be resolved. A clear grasp of this unity in diversity of the body metaphor can save us from all three errors. It is the church as a diversified yet unified body that fulfills its purpose in worship and ministry.

What relationship then is implied between the so-called laity and clergy in the body figure? We must first eradicate the error of interpreting the laity from the standpoint of the clergy; e.g. the clergy does, the laity does not. Rather, we must define the clergy in relation to the body,[6] i.e. the laity are the whole people of God and the clergy are given the privilege of oversight, shepherding, equipping them for service. This we discussed in chapter 1. Several figures may be helpful here to show the proper relationship. Elton Trueblood likens the clergyman to the coach of a football team. The coach instructs, teaches, motivates, and helps direct the play, but the team (the laity) has the major role in actually playing the game. Or perhaps we can see the minister as a filling station attendant. The layman gets his car filled up with fuel and kept in repair by the man at the station. But the layman does the actual running of the car, not the attendant or mechanics. At the same time, the minister is a Christian too! By virtue of that fact he must also "play the game" and "drive the car." But this is essentially because he is a Christian, not simply because he is a clergyman. In other words, he is the helper and equipper of the layman so that the layman can get on with the job, not vice versa as is so often the case. As Stott has told us, "if anybody belongs to anybody in the church, it is not the laity who belongs to the clergy, but the clergy who belongs to the laity." [7] With this relationship in the diversified but integrated body, the work can go forward effectively. It is to this end and principle we need to give our earnest attention.

If such is the relationship in the body, a significant responsibility in the pastoral equipping of the laity for mission is eminently implied.

The Place of Christian Education in Outreach

It is evident that if these principles are taken seriously and implemented, something of a revolution will take place in most congregations. To move the layman out of his comfortable pew and into the arena of evangelism is no mean undertaking. It will first of all take motivation. Years of relative inactivity on the part of the average church member will not be changed easily. And it would seem that the basic responsibility, under God, to motivate these Christians is the pastor's charge.

But let us assume there are already a number of members in the local church who are willing to undertake active service in the call to evangelize. The next demanding task is to begin the educational process that will equip God's people for their ministry. The Lambeth Conference made the following appeal: "No one wants untrained troops. . . . We need a Christian education explosion comparable to that in the secular world." Then it was resolved: "The Conference believes that there is an urgent need for increase in the quantity and quality of training available for lay people for their task in the world." [8] It is apt for one to conclude that Christian education is perhaps one of the most single pressing needs in our churches today if we are to begin evangelizing effectively. I use the term "Christian education" in a very broad, inclusive sense. It refers to the entire "equipping of the saints for the work of the ministry" (Eph. 4:12).

An Adequate Christian Education Program

As a churchwide educational program is undertaken, several elements must be recognized as essential to an adequate structure. First, a valid and comprehensive objective of Christian education is needed.[9] Roger L. Shinn gives the three objects of Christian education based on Mark 12:29-31: (1) to grow in relation to God; (2) to develop trustful and responsible relations with others; and (3) to become a whole person.[10] Without some such basic principles as a goal and basis for education, few Christians will ever become equipped to engage successfully in outreach.

Second, the content of Christian education must be as comprehensive as God's redemptive purpose for man. Revealed truth forms the foundation of the curriculum, and such truth must be presented in real life settings. It sets forth the meaning and demands of discipleship today. Above all, it presents God as redeeming contemporary man in his Son through the agency of the church.

Third, as implied above, an adequate Christian education program must grow out of the needs of man where he is in today's world. The great temptation in Christian education is to become too much "content-centered" as over against "person-centered," i.e. to be so concerned about what we teach that we almost ignore who we teach and why. It is people that matter so much to God.

Fourth, the function of Christian education should help persons fulfill God's intention for them. This is implied in the entire concept of Christian teaching. This idea will be expanded as we discuss the actual nature of accomplishing one's ministry in the life of outreach.

Finally, Christian education must be seen more broadly than just equipping the church for its task—central and vital as that is. It must be broad enough to reach out into the unbelieving community also and confront people with God's revealed truth. Jesus the teacher is an obvious example of this principle. A. Leonard Griffith has well said, "He challenges us, this man outside the church. . . . He challenges us to reach him and commend our faith to him. He challenges us simply because he is there just as Mount Everest challenged adventurous men until they finally conquered it." [11] And to carry the simile on, if the local church made the preparation and effort in its Christian education program of outreach in as dedicated a fashion as Sir Edmund Hillary and his party did in their conquering of Mount Everest, the results would be similar.

Such a comprehensive Christian education program obviously calls for mature and imaginative leadership; a leadership that may exist only in the pastor and a few members at the moment. It is very evident that in many congregations leaders will have to be trained before the real task of educating the bulk of the laity can even begin. This is so often painfully true. Yet this must not deter one from beginning. A start must be made. What then are the qualities we must look for and attempt to create in those who shall lead? One pastor, Rev. R. Rodney Collins, has set forth what is to be sought and developed in leaders:

Qualifications for Leadership

1. A humble dependence on God whose Holy Spirit guides into all the truth (John 16:13). A young married couple leading an interna-

tional Bible study group in a London church confessed, "If we try to do it in our own strength we get flustered and frustrated. We have learned to trust the Lord to help us."

2. A readiness to stir up (2 Tim. 1:6) and not neglect (1 Tim. 4:14) one's gifts.

3. An appreciation of the place of comprehensive Christian education in the Church's life, in accordance with the great commission, "Make disciples . . . teaching them" (the present participle implying a continuous process, not only preparing believers for baptism but continuing afterwards with a view to practical Christian living).

4. Teachability, especially in regard to modern educational techniques and methods. "Give instruction to a wise man and he will be still wiser" (Prov. 9:9, RSV). "You then who teach others, will you not teach yourself?" (Rom. 2:21, RSV).

5. Faithfulness, rather than exceptional ability. "Faithful men . . . will be able to teach others also" (2 Tim. 2:2, RSV).

6. A love of people and a real concern for them, rather than a passion for talking to them!

7. A respect for others which enables one to accept criticism and profit by it (Rom. 12:3).

8. Sensitivity in personal relationships. The good and efficient work of a dedicated leader can be vitiated if his relations with others lack a sensitive awareness of their feelings, needs and desires.

9. The ability to deal with personality problems especially those arising out of the voluntary nature of Christian service.

10. An optimistic spirit inspired by Christian hope which will not easily be depressed by difficulties, disappointments, and discouragements.[12]

These qualifications may seem a large order, and I suppose they are never completely attained by any. Still, worthy goals give direction when taken seriously.

Let us now pause for a moment and summarize what we have been calling for to this point. We are arguing that the entire body of the church has received the commission to evangelize. In this light, the laity must be equipped for the task. Hence we have stressed the importance and nature of Christian education. But before the mass of church members can be taught, leaders—mature leaders—must be developed in order that they may adequately teach others. The overriding implication is that the pastor is the one who must "get the ball rolling." If such is to be the immediate goal, the pastor must recognize the necessity of his giving himself, at least to some extent, to what is commonly called church administration and programming.

Church Administration and Organization in Mission

Administration seems to be a bad word for some pastors. "Is it not outside the minister's spiritual call?" pastors often ask. It is easy to be just a bit super-pious on this point and hold that ministers are to give themselves only to the "spiritual" aspects of ministry, letting the deacons or stewards or lay leaders handle the mundane things like administration. Is such an attitude justifiable? I seriously doubt it. Maybe it will help us if we can come to realize just what church administration is. Lindgren defines it in these words:

> Purposeful church administration is the involvement of the church in the discovery of her nature and mission and in moving in a coherent and comprehensive manner toward providing such experience as will enable the church to utilize all her resources and personnel in the fulfillment of her mission of making known God's love for all men.[13]

That hardly sounds "unspiritual"! Surely a pastor can see his responsibilities there. Even a secular definition of administration has significant implications for a church when its principles are translated into the life of a Christian congregation. For example, Ordway Tead tells us:

> Administration is the process and agency which is responsible for the determination of the aims for which an organization and its management are to strive, which establishes the broad policies under which they are to operate, and which gives general oversight to the continuing effectiveness of the total operation in reaching the objectives sought.[14]

If one understands the nature and objectives of mission even this is not "unspiritual" for God's ministers. W. L. Howse has well stated:

> For years many leaders have felt that administration was fine for the business world but that it was too secular for churches. The

> recognition of administration as a church process will remove the stigma of secularism and make administration a useful tool for churches. Good administration is nothing more than following correct processes in getting essential work done well.[15]

Having been a pastor myself for many years, I finally came to the conclusion—somewhat reluctantly I must admit—that serious church administration is a responsibility of the pastor. It is a responsibility he cannot avoid. It is one he should not want to escape. To a greater or lesser degree, he actually does it anyway. Therefore, he should do it well. It does not seem "spiritual" at all to me to engage in this or any part of the ministry in a half-hearted, negligent manner. If God has entrusted to a pastor a leadership role in the church, administration is vital and inescapable. For the sake of the Kingdom he should do it well—very well and with zest. It is a part of the ministry in today's kind of world. I am not calling on pastors to become sanctified "wheeler-dealers." But let's face reality: in our contemporary, technologically-oriented society and in the face of the vital needs of developing a dynamic educational program in the local church, the spiritually-minded pastor cannot sidestep his responsibilities in the area of church administration and programming.

In the light of the need and call for good church administration, George Wilson has set out three important principles:

> 1. Administration exists to accomplish something—in this case, the work of the church or work which the church designates. The main question which the church must face in this regard is not whether or not it will have administration. The question the church faces in this regard is a choice of good versus bad administration. Any attempt to get anything done through the efforts of others is administration of some kind. The question is, what kind?
>
> 2. Objectives and commensurate goals are indispensable to good administration. Timeless intention to act, coupled with specific actions planned in such a light help the church to shape being out of co-operative chaos, i.e. mutually created by competing organizations.

> 3. People are central. A writer has stated, "Leadership is measured by the led." There is no progress if people do not make progress. Study of the biblical documents is not planned as an exercise for computers or machines, but for persons. Training to minister in Christ's name—to go "to him outside the camp, bearing the stigma he bore" (Heb. 13:14, NEB)—is not a task designed to be accomplished by empty classrooms or sanctuaries, but by people committed to ministering in the world.[16]

Thus the minister begins the task of "equipping the saints for the work of the ministry" (Eph. 4:12). But what are the structures of ministry that are to be created? To this important issue we must now address ourselves.

"Gifts of the Spirit" and Organization for Ministry

Perhaps the reason church administration has often seemed a little tedious is because of the problem of finding a really satisfying way to organize the local church into effective ministry. It so often appears that one is organizing merely for organization's sake and taking quite a humanistic approach in so doing. There is little satisfaction in organizing a church simply to keep the machine ticking over. We may even feel at times that our church programming is a mere manipulating of people. The results thus seem to be that we are forever putting square pegs in round holes and no one is genuinely satisfied and the work suffers. I am convinced, however, there is a pattern that can be employed that is deeply rooted in the Scriptures and in the dynamic of the Holy Spirit's working among his people. If such be the case, satisfaction and success can be expected. I refer to the biblical principle which Paul in particular labored to implement in the churches he founded, namely that of Christians serving in the context of the "gifts of the Spirit"—the *charismata.*

I must be frank and confess that in approaching such a theme, it is done with some hesitation; I fear misunderstanding. The biblical concept of gifts is often grossly misinterpreted—especially is this so today. Perversions of the teaching have left few churches untouched. Also, there is always the danger of being "labeled." Labels are usually quite emotive—to the extent that at times some may even be tempted to throw out the baby with the bath water. But I trust neither of these apprehensions will be evoked by what I wish to say on this most important issue. Perhaps the single most important fact to realize as we take up this theme is that these gifts of the Spirit are given to the church for ministry. They are not for individual, spiritual indulgence of any kind. The Holy Spirit imparts them essentially so that believers may be effective in their service for Christ. If we keep this principle before us we can keep ourselves from many errors.

Here is a biblical teaching that is just beginning to be discussed in the contemporary church—at least in a positive, constructive manner. Yet it had significant prominence in the life and ministry in the early church. Three rather lengthy passages are devoted to the theme in Paul's writings: Ephesians 4:4-16; 1 Corinthians 12—14; Romans 12:3-8. A number of things need to be said concerning the concept.

The New Testament declares that when Christ ascended back to the Father, he " 'led a host of captives and he gave gifts to men' " (Eph. 4:8). These gifts are the consequence of the presence of the "Spirit of promise" who indwells all believers. As previously stated, they are given by our Lord for the purpose of equipping his people for the work of the ministry. It is important to distinguish these gifts of the Spirit from the fruits of the Spirit (Gal. 5:22-24). The fruits are the manifestation of the Spirit in the daily life of the Christian to make him Christlike in character. The gifts are the manifestation of the Spirit through the believer to make his service effective. In a word, they are "ministering gifts."

Spiritual gifts are enumerated in the three primary New Testament passages mentioned above. First, in Ephesians 4:11 we have the following:

1. Apostles
2. Prophets
3. Evangelists
4. Pastors
5. Teachers

Then Romans 12:3-8 presents some additions:

1. Prophecy
2. Ministrations
3. Teacher
4. Exhortation
5. Giver
6. Ruler
7. He who shows mercy

Finally, we read in 1 Corinthians 12:8-10:

1. Utterance of wisdom
2. Utterance of knowledge
3. Faith
4. Healing
5. Miracles
6. Prophecy
7. Discernment of spirits
8. Varieties of tongues
9. Interpretations of tongues

It is quite evident from the above that the principle of the gifts of the Spirit has singular importance for the entire work of the ministry. Therefore, it cannot be taken lightly by the church. Paul says, "It is important, brethren, that you should have clear knowledge on the subject of spiritual gifts" (1 Cor. 12:1, Weymouth). What can be said about these gifts? Initially, it is clear that some gifts are obviously the Christians themselves with particular ministries, e.g. apostles, prophets, teachers, etc. In other cases the emphasis is upon the gift itself rather than the individual who is gifted, e.g. faith, varieties of tongues, and so on. Yet this distinction should not be pressed too far. Perhaps the simplest thing to say is that a gift apart from a believer to exercise the gift is an abstraction, and a believer must have a gift to be an effective Christian servant. The gift and the gifted form the warp and woof of the theme.

Further, the gifts of the Spirit are not to be confused with natural talents. Though most have some natural abilities—abilities that God will surely use in his service—the spiritual gifts are not these *per se.* Marcus Dods points this out by stating, "They [the believers] were endowed at their conversion . . . with certain powers which they had not previously possessed, and which were due to the influence of the Holy Spirit." [17]

Then the gifts must be seen as spiritual powers that the believer must exercise only under the control of the Holy Spirit. They are not to be used simply when and how the believer wishes, let alone to enjoy selfishly. Alfred Plummer declares, "The Operator . . . is always God: every one of the gifts in every person that manifests them . . . is bestowed and set in motion by Him." [18] It is quite obvious that Paul wrote the lengthy passage found in 1 Corinthians 12—14 to direct the use of the gifts and to save the church from just such abuses.

To summarize, the gifts must be understood as a grace-gift, a supernatural endowment, a spiritual manifestation of God the Spirit through the believer for: (1) the enrichment of the body and (2) for the development and work of the ministry. As has been said, "It is simply the Holy Spirit working through us in a given manner, at the time he, the Spirit, chooses, for the carrying out of the ministry to which we have been appointed of God." [19] E. P. Gould states, "They are all, however various, to be employed in the service of him, the one Lord." [20] Moreover, it must be emphasized that the Holy Spirit distributes gifts to every believer. Paul seems to state that there are no exceptions—every believer has a gift or gifts apportioned to him. Lenski declares that the emphasis rests primarily on the dative in 1 Corinthians 12:7, implying that "to each one

. . . each believer has his gifts, and every bestowal of a gift is for the common good".[21]

At this point it is important that we understand the actual meaning of each gift and the purpose for which it is intended. Perhaps the following general classification will help:

1. For the proclamation of God's self-disclosure: the gift of prophecy or preaching.
2. For teaching the divine revelation: the gift of teaching.
3. For enabling God's blessing to flow into needy lives: the gift of faith that enables believers to rest upon God's promises and trust in the power that is beyond the sphere of human possibilities.
4. For the revelation of God's will and purpose in matters: the gift of wisdom so that God's purpose in his word can be grasped.
5. For understanding the practical application of eternal principles in daily experience: the utterance of knowledge.
6. For protection against evil: the gift of discernment of spirits.
7. For the practical manifestation of the love of Christ there are three gifts: mercy, the Paraclete gift and giving.
8. For maintaining order in the life and work of the church: the gift of government. [This is surely not far from what we have been speaking about when we discussed the importance of church administration.]
9. For help in the community: the gift of serviceable ministries or "helps."
10. As special signs of God's power and presence, there are four gifts: miracles, healings, tongues, and interpretations of tongues.[22]

A few things must be said concerning this brief outline of the gifts. First, the number of gifts found in the Scriptures is comparatively small. This leads to the conclusion that each gift listed must be understood as a designation of a class of gifts. In each classification there will quite naturally be many variations. Circumstances, situations, and needs vary from culture to culture and from generation to generation. There are probably hundreds of individual, specific gifts. The biblical gifts must be seen as flexible in their manifestations so as to meet the relevant needs of all people at all times.

Also, a study of all the gifts of the Spirit make it evident that God has provided in full measure for all needs of the church in its growth, worship, and ministry. The organization of the local church, its government, its instruction and equipping, its worship, its ministry of witness, and its entire corporate life of ministry are fully cared for. As John Short has said: "Let there be among the Corinthian Christians, and in every Christian church in any age, clear recognition of the simple truth that in such a divinely appointed organism as the body of Christ, for its vitality and its effective witness, a variety of functions is required." [23] And the Spirit will surely see to it that no part of work suffers for lack of a gift if the church is open to his lead.

Furthermore, the principle of spiritual gifts is what truly makes the local church a body. G. G. Findlay points out that the *charismata* of the Spirit are "portioned out amongst the members of Christ, for manifold and reciprocal service to His body." [24] Paul set the whole theme in this important context. The Holy Spirit bestows these gifts "as he wills" (1 Cor. 12:11, RSV). Surely he will not create a body that is all hands or eyes or feet or tongues. That would be a monstrosity, not a body at all. He will develop a perfectly functioning and unified body. I am convinced that a church never becomes a unified whole by mere organization alone. It is the Spirit who creates the body. Barclay states in commenting on the Corinthian church, "The whole idea of Paul . . . is to stress the essential unity of the church." [25]

Finally, it is when *the whole church* employs their gifts under the direction of the Holy Spirit that the church is built up and strengthened and the work progresses and the *missio Dei* is carried on. It should be stressed again right here that every member will *not* have the same gift in mission. Not every Christian will necessarily be a great soul-winner, for example. But as the entire church exercises its specific gifts, the whole witnessing body—all members must witness even if all are not gifted soul-winners—makes a *unified* impact for Christ. It is corporate influence more than individual impact that matters most. As Lenski has said, "each member of the church benefits the entire body by rightly employing his *particular* gift." [26] The work is God's mission, and it is quite clear in the New Testament that the work is energized by the Spirit through the *whole gifted church.* That is where the stress lies.

We cannot undertake here a detailed exegesis of the important passages on spiritual gifts although such a study would be tremendously helpful. But perhaps it has now been made clear by this short discussion on the theme that, as Barclay says, when a church functions on the basis of the gifts of the Spirit, "The picture we get is the picture of a Church vividly alive. Things happened; in fact astonishing things happened. Life was heightened and intensified and sensitized. There was nothing flat and dull and ordinary about the . . . Church." [27] This is what we all desire today for the body, and what we must see if we are to evangelize our contemporary generation.

In the light of all that has been said concerning spiritual gifts, here is the suggestion I wish to put forward: the church should be geared in its organizational life so that the members of the church can exercise the gifts that have been committed to them by the Holy Spirit. It may be that this is already being done to a greater or lesser degree *implicitly.* But what is being called for is an *explicit* structuring of the organizational pattern of the local church along these lines. In other words, the church's program should be developed in such a manner that the Holy Spirit can manifest himself in and through his people as he wills. This obviously calls for a number of revolutionary approaches.

Initially, we must move toward placing far more confidence in our gifted church members. As a layman has expressed it:

> Why is it the Church today will not trust its members? Why does the Church so often decline to recognize and to accept the activity of the Spirit among unregulated groups of Christians? Why is all initiative in the Church expected and presumed to derive from the clergy? It is because we have substituted for the biblical doctrine of the Holy Spirit as ruler in the Church, a doctrine of our own,

> unknown to scripture, the authority of professionalism. In regard to the conducting of services and the administration of the sacraments the authority of the ministry is not in question. But we are now considering the training and commissioning of Christian men and women to take lay initiative in the world.[28]

If we take seriously the lay-centered ministry concept and genuinely believe that God's Spirit empowers and gives gifts to all Christians, we must trust these believers to get on with the job. After all, is not this what we mean by the priesthood of all believers? And it is more than merely incidental that such an approach saves the layman from feeling so inadequate for the task and responsibility that is clearly his. When he recognizes he has a gift and he is led to discover it, he is motivated as never before. He can never again excuse himself by saying, "I have no talents." Even if that is true, *he has a gift* and is therefore adequate and responsible to serve Christ.

As already stated, there will probably be quite a change in the present structures of the local church program. I do not mean a little change here and there or merely using more pop tunes in the services or the preacher using "groovy" talk when he preaches. I am suggesting a real revolution that organizes a church on the basis of what spiritual gifts are manifest and what needs to surface in the corporate life of the body rather than just trying to prop up old, irrelevant, inept structures. In the concluding section of this chapter some guidelines on how to implement this principle will be considered.

Moreover, as discussed earlier, much instruction, Christian teaching, and help must be given to implement the principle. Most Christians are grossly ignorant concerning the work of the Holy Spirit. I should suppose the bulk of God's people do not even know Christians are gifted by the Holy Spirit, let alone know what gifts the Spirit would manifest through them. A real process of education on pneumatology is usually needed as the gifts will need sharpening and developing. It may well be that many misconceptions concerning the work of the Holy Spirit will have to be eradicated. The minister must be on guard to protect his people from being swept away in some movement that reports itself to be of the Holy Spirit but, though it may speak much of particular gifts of the Spirit, bears little fruit of the Spirit. It is all too clear that not a few Christians have fallen victim to gross errors concerning the *charismata* of the Spirit. As Paul was on guard for the believers in Corinth, so also must be the contemporary pastor.

Naturally the minister will have to give himself to the development and administration of these new goals. Changing basic approaches and structures will be difficult. But these changes seem mandatory, and although the pastor may be somewhat reluctant to give himself to the increased administrative responsibilities of developing new programs, I see no other way out.

So there it is! The *missio Dei* committed to the whole body; and the layman, recognizing that he is gifted by the Spirit, engages in ministry. He now needs church structures through which he can serve in relation to his specific gifts and meeting specific needs. He desperately needs development through Christian education. And the pastor stands as the layman's servant to see that he gets it all. Thus the church becomes a truly unified, functioning body being built up in the faith, and the *missio Dei* goes forward. Sounds great! But can it work?

Some Practical Suggestions

Let me say that I believe what we find in the Scriptures by way of principle can be implemented pragmatically in the local church. If God has called all of his people into mission, then I believe God's people can be led to perform the task. In this closing section we will consider some practical suggestions on how to develop a church-centered evangelistic program. It calls for honesty and bravery, but it must be undertaken. This most pastors deeply feel; as a pastor friend of mine once said, "The world will not be won by people who stand around wringing their hands." We have bewailed the condition of the church long enough. We have diagnosed our ills until one feels almost like a spiritual hypochondriac. The call is for action, even if it is only a beginning. The suggestions I wish to make may be a mere beginning, but they have been undertaken by others and God has honored the honest effort. At least it is a start.

From the standpoint of the corporate service of the church, we must be willing right at the start to face the fact that perhaps many of the present structures of church life will need changing. We have talked about it for a long time. But how can it be done? That is the crunch! We all know only too well that there is always resistance—often strong resistance—to change. Therefore, I suggest initially that the pastor who is keenly aware of the needs gather around himself a group of spiritual church leaders. It would be best in most instances to have a representative group from the structured life of the church, i.e. the directors of the various departmental aspects of the church program. But above all, let them be the ones who are spiritually minded and open to the purposes of God in mission. I think it vital to choose no one but spiritually perceptive people even if only a few are available. I do not mean to imply we are to be judges of how well our church members are related to God. But one can usually discern those who are open to the moving of the Holy Spirit. Then the pastor should begin with this group; teaching, encouraging, challenging, and informing them concerning the need of evangelism and the openness that is required if the church is going to be effectively geared for outreach. They should be made vividly aware of what the actual goals and mission of the church are. It is essential and foundational to know where we want to go. So often the church keeps merely ticking over because it has no real goals. As has been facetiously said, if you have no goal, you will hit it every time.

Then after much prayer, education, and heart-searching, when the pastor feels his group is genuinely committed to mission and zealous for it, they should sit down together with their goals before them and scrutinize the entire present church program. Let them examine and evaluate each and every facet of the structured life of the church. Let them be honest about each phase, asking these questions: Does it line up with the goals of the church? Does it really have relevance for today's world? Does it honestly meet needs? Does it genuinely further the kingdom of God through the life of the church? Does it accord with scriptural principles, such as the exercising of spiritual gifts? These are not easy questions to ask. They call for objectivity, integrity, and not a little courage. We all have vested interests in our present church program, and to be objective and honest is often painful. But I see it as essential that we analyze what we are doing in the light of what we, under God, *should* be doing. In the appendix of this book a guide for conducting such a survey is given. Many churches have followed such an approach and have found it very helpful.

Now if the answers to these questions can be given in such a way that we can unqualifiedly say that a certain part of the church program lines up with scriptural goals and principles, then it is ridiculous to change that phase of the program, let alone throw it out. Change for change's sake alone is unworthy. But if it becomes clear, as it often does, that certain programs are archaic, outmoded, irrelevant, and not meeting the needs—thus superfluous to mission—then let us be honest and courageous enough to change them. In other words, if it is dead, give it a decent burial.

All we have said to this point is negative and rather destructive, but there is a positive side to the issue. There is a constructive work to be done. After a careful diagnosis of the present structures and the tentative (I emphasize *tentative*) elimination of the irrelevant, then there must begin the rebuilding of a positive, relevant, and dynamic new church program. Two vital principles must be kept in mind in this endeavor; (1) the church's goals must be clearly before the group, and (2) the new structures must be built on the principle of involving all church members, allowing them to exercise their gifts. And we must remember that our structures are to be geared to prepare for our mission in the world. This implies that we must give attention to "go structures" more than "come structures," at least as far as evangelistic outreach is concerned. This will obviously take much prayer, thought, and time. It will be demanding on the pastor and the mission action group. I think it wise in most situations for all this negative and positive work on the church program to be done in closed committee, at least in the earlier stages. Often the whole church at the outset is not ready for drastic changes. But after a tentative new church program is developed, the task of educating the church must be undertaken.

Of course, the educational process will be going on all during this initial spade work. What is vital to recognize is that the church must be informed and inspired concerning mission and what is needed to fulfill the commission. Here patience, perseverance, understanding, and love must be the keynote. Christians move slowly—some will not move at all. Yet with the leadership and power of the Holy Spirit, the church can be challenged, educated, and inspired to follow the Spirit's leading into a new church structure geared for outreach.

It cannot be emphasized too strongly that the educational process must be patiently followed. It is bound to take time. Perhaps months and even years may be necessary in some churches. But it must be done for the sake of mission. Of course, there will be those in the church who will not buy it at any cost. What do we do then? In love, and I underline *in love*, they must be bypassed for the work to go on. Mission is vital, and if there are those who stand in the way, they must be understood and loved but dealt with as our Lord himself did.

Such an approach to church programming also demands insight into community needs. I would suggest that a careful survey of the community as well as of the church itself be undertaken by the action group. Issues such as the special sociological aspects of the community to which the church hopes to minister must be grasped and understood. The group should come alive to the specific needs of their particular community. The geographical area and its influences on church life should be considered. We need to know the general characteristics of those whom we are attempting to reach, i.e. what is their social, educational, financial status or level, and so on. We must become far more conscious of the sociological aspects of mission.

Furthermore, the tentative program that is to be implemented must be kept flexible. Some new programs attempted may prove quite unsuccessful when they are actually executed. If such be the case, let us be brave once again and change them and try something else. The mistake of getting wedded to the new program can be as deadly as being wedded to the old. It must be remembered it is not a sin to fail, the sin lies in never attempting anything lest one should fail. The local church must be subject to constant change in its programming for mission if it is to improve its methodologies and keep abreast of the ever-changing community.

Up to now we have obviously been discussing that which relates essentially to the structured, corporate life of the church. There is much that the individual members can do—and should be led to do. What is vital at this point is this principle for the pastor-evangelist in developing his church for mission. He may have to begin with very few interested leaders, but here is something he *can* do. As already mentioned, it has been undertaken in many congregations and has done quite successfully. Now let us look at the more important areas of outreach and present a few case studies to illustrate how effective some of these new methodologies are.

Some Practical Examples

The principle of group dynamics should be investigated. The upsurge of interest in small groups, e.g. house groups, Bible study groups, young people's groups, retreats, has proved most useful. The church that overlooks this field of mission endeavor and church edification is ignoring a vast reservoir of productive blessing. A few examples of success in these fields of innovative outreach may prove helpful.

As most of us know, one of the most exciting new methods of outreach is the house group. Of course, it is not new as a principle. It can be traced right back to the New Testament. But a new impetus has been given to it lately. Many churches have implemented the idea into very fruitful endeavors. Paul Tucker who serves a very difficult inner-city area has had unusual success with this approach. There are several lay people in this church who have a regular program of house meetings. Some of the members have actually moved from their comfortable surburban homes to live in the inner-city area so as to open their homes and minister. The leaders keep their homes open at all times (this seems important), and then once a week they have a structured group meeting. A regular, solid attendance has been built up. They have learned to be very flexible and not to be shocked or put off by what they experience from those who attend. They have communicated to their attenders, and to the entire community for that matter, that they truly care. As a result they have little difficulty in attracting the pure "outsider" into their homes. Periodically the various leaders meet and are instructed by the pastor and share together their experiences. Pastor Tucker readily admits that these house groups are one of the most effective methods the church utilizes to contact and win the unbeliever. If such an approach can be successful in a very difficult inner-city area, one is led to believe it would work almost anywhere. All it takes is dedication and instructed lay people. And there is a wealth of material provided on how to conduct such groups.

Then, young people's work must be given a fresh look. One thing is certain in this field of ministry: conventional methodologies will not reach multitudes of young people today—especially young people whose families are totally unchurched. It is quite clear that church members, and especially youth leaders, must learn to accept young people as they are and let them express themselves in their own way. If their music, dress, and language are strange to the older generation, it does not necessarily mean they are wrong. And young people are open to the gospel in a fashion not experienced for many years. Young people are asking serious questions today. Let us be open, imaginative, and zealous in reaching them. If it takes unusual things to reach them, may the church be mature enough to employ such methods. Much success has been had in this entire area by imaginative churches and their leaders.

Some of my theological students brought real innovations in behalf of young people in churches where they ministered. They found that two or three methods were quite effective. First, there is coffeehouse work. At one church a group of our young men led the young people of the congregation into a coffeehouse program. A room was found, and it was "decorated"—at least I suppose one could call it that. The rather drab old room was suddenly made alive with psychedelic walls and wild music. When the church's young people got the word around the community that a coffeehouse was functioning, the outside young people came in droves. This is often the case. Our mature young men trained the church young people to witness, and as a result many from the outside came to find Christ. This is surely what evangelism is all about.

In the same geographical area the students planned a gospel concert. Here is another real possibility for effective outreach. They rented a local civic hall—a neutral hall seems important for this kind of venture. Two Christian pop groups were enlisted, and word went out in the area as to what was to take place. Tickets were sold; young people today feel that if anything is worthwhile you have to pay for it. The night of the concert saw the hall well filled with young people from all walks of life. As I sat there and heard the music, saw the clever skits that our men wrote and presented, and recognized that the gospel was genuinely being communicated, I realized you could never get that many unchurched young people into a regular church service to give them the good news in the conventional way. And any church can develop a gospel concert program. If a pastor thinks he cannot, let him ask a few of his own young people. They will usually get the idea implemented. Many are just waiting for an opportunity to reach others in the ways they know are effective.

What has been said previously about small groups has an obvious application to young people. Time would fail to tell of the exciting things I have seen when young people are brought together as a group to learn more of Christ. Church after church is turning its younger members loose and letting them develop their groups.

Then there is the bus ministry that has been used very effectively by many churches. Much material has been written on this outreach methodology. Space precludes discussing its details here. Every church should investigate the possibility.

Further, a geriatrics program offers many opportunities. So many older people are isolated and lonely. Especially is this true in the larger metropolitan areas. They cry for recognition. A report was given on London television recently that some older citizens are so cut off and alone that the only people they relate to are television personalities, and they will actually kiss the TV receiver when the face of their favorite appears. This should cause the church to do some real heart-searching—and maybe some genuine repenting.

An interesting program for senior citizens has been undertaken by the Walnut Street Baptist Church in Louisville, Kentucky. They have built a high-rise to house elderly, retired people. Seeing the pressing need for accommodation and a sense of belonging, the church ventured into this ambitious scheme and has successfully brought it into being. Financing is not the problem one might at first suppose. The monies can usually be secured and the program remains solvent. It certainly does not require a wealthy church to undertake such a plan. And it is obviously a tremendous ministry to the elderly.

In my last pastorate we did several things for the older people of the community. We discovered it takes so little to be of help to these people. And when one sees the joy and happiness one spreads by working with these folk, it certainly makes every effort worthwhile. Trips were planned for them. A regular visitation by the laymen was instituted. Social times at the church were a regular occurrence. Many activities can be conceived. These lonely people desperately need our love and care. Almost any church could develop a senior citizens club of its own. It would mean much to many and could be used by God to reach people for Christ.

Every community has its own special peculiar needs. Delinquency, crime, drugs, illegitimacy, minority groups, underprivileged areas, the isolated wealthy, needy subcultural groups—all these and many other needs can be discovered. The local church should attempt to step into these gaps and minister. The church must get involved in the life of the community. It has been provincial and insular too long. The world needs to know the church exists and is here to minister.

Then there are the multiplied personal ministries the church members can be educated to perform. Personal witnessing is vital and expected of all. Most of us are aware that personal witnessing is the most effective way to confront people with the gospel. Relatively few unbelievers are attending churches now. Therefore, it is the housewife witnessing to the neighbors, the factory worker speaking about Christ to his friends on the job, the young person giving the good news to school friends who will help make the greatest impact on contemporary society. If only God could open our mouths. On this theme, Wilson Carlile said, "I have got the biggest job I have ever tackled in my life. I am trying to open the mouths of people in the pews." [29] I am almost bold enough to say that either the mouths of God's people will be opened, or we are done for. Yet Christians can be inspired and helped and educated to share their witness. There are a number of effective training plans today, e.g. "Win" schools, Kennedy Plan, Campus Crusade, and many others.

An illustration of what one man can accomplish as a personal witness is the story of M. L. O'Neal. This man was the most effective witness for Christ I have ever known personally. He was not a pastor. He was a layman with limited education; he had to drop out of school at fourteen years of age to go to work to help support the family. He was not a great Bible scholar though he faithfully read his Bible. He was anything but a theologian. His speaking ability was not outstanding. Later in life he became a very successful businessman. But this was not his genius. His most remarkable quality lay in his ability to lead others to faith in Christ. This quality developed out of his ardent passion to win the unconverted. He seized every opportunity to witness. I have seen him bear his testimony in every conceivable context. He would witness to waitresses in restaurants, attendants at filling stations, clerks in stores—wherever he met people. I remember his driving thousands of miles just to witness for Christ.

So skillful was he that he rarely offended anyone. I know for a fact he led literally hundreds to faith in the Lord Jesus Christ. He actually burned out his life in seeking people. He became seriously ill not too long ago, and an operation was mandatory. As he was being prepared for the surgery, he faithfully witnessed to the male nurse who was caring for him. He died a short time later—but what a way to go! His whole life was consumed with this one passion. I suppose a misunderstanding psychiatrist would say he was a compulsive or obsessive personality. But here was one layman, totally committed, and God used him significantly. I know few laymen will ever become that effective, yet many can be led to do far more than they are now attempting. To this equipping, the pastor and church leaders must give themselves.

It would further seem wise for members of the church to engage personally in community affairs. So often a caricature is drawn of the Christian as a rather isolated, strange, unreal character—especially is this true of the pastor. I suppose this is not completely without some foundation in fact; a ghetto mentality has surely invaded segments of the church. But if God's people get involved in community affairs (they are citizens of the country as well as of the kingdom), this image can be altered, and opportunity for outreach and Christian ministry can be found.

May I share a personal illustration of this principle? While serving as pastor of a church near a large university, I became convinced I should involve myself in the life of the university. An opportunity came to work on several committees of the International Center of the university. It was time-consuming and occasionally inconvenient. Frequently my wife and I had to curtail certain other activities that some would have felt more important. But we came in contact with people outside the church as never before. We had the opportunity of ministering to students, leaders, and personalities from all over the world. In this context we were able to bear our witness for Christ. A leader from a non-Christian country visited us on one occasion, and we attempted to entertain him in a hospitable Christian manner. We tried to be a friend to him. We gave him a copy of the New Testament in simple, modern English. He visited our worship services. Before he left our community he had read a large portion of the New Testament and was so impressed with the Christian warmth he had experienced among our church people that he said, "If ever missionaries from your churches want to come to our country, I shall let them in." And he was in the position in his country to do that very thing. We must minister to the world whenever and however we can. We shall never reach people by being walled up in our cloisters.

There are countless opportunities to demonstrate Christ's love in deeds of kindness that Christians can be encouraged and helped to attempt. Wherever there is a need, a Christian can step in. As an example of this type of service I would like to tell of a dear lady in a former pastorate of mine. She was very poor by many standards, and her husband was rather unstable. But she excelled in doing personally helpful things for people. She was never able to do big things—finances prohibited that. Yet she was always doing what she could. She was loved and appreciated for it. Her spirit of genuine Christlikeness in meeting needs as best she could was inspirational. Surely Christians can be led to emulate this principle in their daily lives.

The list could go on, but let the mission action group along with the entire congregation discover what God is leading the church to do, corporately and individually. God is in this world ministering; the church should be there with him. Let us break out of the four walls of our buildings and meet the world. Much material has been produced today to give direction on the suggestions made here and on other approaches as well.

Surely the Holy Spirit will lead the church and its individual members into avenues of mission outreach that will prove effective for God's glory and the winning of men.

Notes

1. Michael Green, *Evangelism in the Early Church*, op. cit., p. 173.
2. Ibid., p. 175.
3. George Goyder, *The People's Church* (London: Hodder and Stoughton, 1966), p. 9.
4. Quoted in J. A. T. Robinson's work, *The Layman's Church*, p. 10.
5. John R. W. Stott, *One People* (London: Falcon Books, 1969), p. 24.
6. Ibid., p. 47.
7. Ibid., p. 47.
8. Ibid., p. 54.
9. This and the following main points are from an unpublished paper presented by A. V. Washburn at the Baptist World Alliance Conference on Teaching and Training, Tokyo, July 12-18, 1970.
10. Roger L. Shinn, *The Educational Mission of Our Church* (Philadelphia, United Press, 1962), pp. 66-7.
11. A. Leonard Griffith, *What Is a Christian?* (Nashville: Abingdon Press, 1961), pp. 117-20.
12. From an unpublished paper presented by the Rev. Rodney Collins at the Baptist World Alliance Conference on Teaching and Training, Tokyo, 1970.
13. Alvin J. Lindgren, *Foundations for Purposeful Church Administration* (Nashville: Abingdon Press, 1965), p. 60.
14. Ordway Tead, *The Art of Administration* (New York: McGraw-Hill, 1951), p. 101.

15. Quoted from an unpublished paper presented by the Rev. George Wilson, Jr. at the Baptist World Alliance Conference on Teaching and Training, Tokyo, 1970.
16. Ibid.
17. *The Expositor's Bible,* 1 Corinthians (London: Hodder and Stoughton, 1891), p. 278.
18. *The International Critical Commentary,* 1 Corinthians (Edinburgh: T. & T. Clark), p. 264.
19. Alexander Rattray Hay, *The New Testament Order for Church and Missionary* (New Testament Missionary Union, 1947), p. 177.
20. *An American Commentary,* vol. v (Philadelphia: The American Baptist Publication Society, 1887), p. 104.
21. R. C. H. Lenski, *The Interpretation of St. Paul's First and Second Epistles to the Corinthians* (Minneapolis: Augsburg Publishing House, 1937), pp. 496-7.
22. Alexander Rattray Hay, op. cit., p. 186.
23. *The Interpreter's Bible,* vol. 10 (Nashville: Abingdon Press, 1953), p. 164.
24. *The Expositor's Greek Testament,* vol. 2 (Grand Rapids: Eerdman's Publishing Co., 1951), p. 887.
25. William Barclay, *Letters to the Corinthians* (Philadelphia: Westminster Press, 1954), p. 120.
26. R. C. H. Lenski, op. cit., p. 497, (italics mine).
27. William Barclay, op. cit., p. 124.
28. George Goyder, op. cit., p. 35.
29. Quoted in John R. W. Stott, *Our Guilty Silence* (London: Hodder and Stoughton, 1967), p. 13.

4 The Preaching of the Pastor-Evangelist

At a recent conference for theological teachers, we heard a lecture from a professor of education on the inadequacies of the lecture method of teaching. After the rather self-contradictory hour was over, one of my colleagues asked our lecturer privately if what he said about lecturing in the classroom applied to preaching in the church. The professor retorted that though he was a lay preacher and preached every Sunday, so convinced was he of the irrelevance of formally addressing people that he felt the hour spent each Sunday listening to a sermon was a waste of time.

What the distinguished professor of education felt concerning preaching is not an uncommon attitude today. Even though there seems to be a revival of new interest in preaching, never before in the history of the church has the preaching enterprise been so seriously called into question—at least in some circles. Douglas Stewart tells us:

> Preaching as such has fallen into disregard if not into disrepute. To localize this fact one could easily construct a historic chain of dominant London preachers from John Donne to Charles Haddon Spurgeon, who generation after generation, in their immensely varied traditions, shaped and influenced the life of London. But somewhere, between Spurgeon and ourselves, the chain is broken.[1]

Yet this is only to be expected, the antagonists of preaching declare. After all, their arguments run, are we not in the television age? What is called for is something new if we are to communicate to men today. Forthright proclamation of the truth is out. Dialogue is now in vogue. The uneasy mind of modern man demands pictures, involvement, discussion, etc. In the light of such widespread feelings, it is small wonder that a leading churchman has said that "preaching is in the doldrums, if not in the dog-house." [2] A classic example of the current mood is seen in the fact that once the motto of Glasgow was: "Let Glasgow flourish through the preaching of the Word." Today the same city has on its promotional material simply "Let Glasgow flourish." What has happened to the preaching of the Word?

If what has been said about preaching in general be true, it is especially true of evangelistic preaching in particular. Today many feel that "preaching the gospel" as we traditionally understand that phrase is almost an irrelevant exercise. Why preach evangelistically to those who are already evangelized, it is often asked. Relatively few of those who need to hear the good news ever come to the church services, we are told. Even those who still believe in preaching or serve in a context where preaching is traditionally primary seem to contradict their position if one could judge by the amount of time and effort they give each week to developing great pulpit ministry. They often let all other demands of ministry crowd out pulpit preparation, and one wonders how serious they really are about their plea for the primacy of preaching. But such an attitude was far from the case until quite recent times.

The History of Preaching

The preaching enterprise has an illustrious history. As far back as Old Testament times, the preaching prophets stood head and shoulders above other men. Hear Elijah thundering out judgment upon Israel until even Ahab quaked! See the tearful Jeremiah preaching with such influence that finally Zedekiah permitted him to be cast into a pit in order to stop his voice! Or look at Elisha boldly addressing King Jehoram as he tells the monarch to send Naaman to him that all may know there is a prophet in Israel! And time fails one to relate the thrilling stories that grow out of the preaching of Amos, Isaiah, the mystical Ezekiel, and their fellow-prophets.

Viewing the old dispensation, one thing is certain and stands out in bold relief: The preaching of the prophets had a profound influence on every aspect of the Israelite nation.

The New Testament era saw no change in emphasis; preaching remained paramount. In fact, preaching came into its own in the apostolic age. Preaching in the early church was central to the divine mission. Who could deny, for example, the centrality and profound influence of the preaching of John the Baptist? All Jerusalem went out into the desert to hear him. Look into the ministry of the Lord himself! Ker has said, "The great work of Christ during his life was preaching." [3] Perhaps this is to overstate the case, but it is obvious that preaching was a very significant part of Jesus' ministry. Our Lord's own testimony was that he came "to bear witness to the truth" (John 18:37, RSV). It was natural, therefore, that the apostles and early disciples would follow the same tradition. Whether it was Peter at Pentecost, Philip in Samaria, or Paul in philosophical Athens, the power of proclamation was skillfully employed.

The church fathers were no exception to the rule; they too were great preachers. One still marvels at the impact of men like Origen, Clement, and others. So it was through centuries of church history. It was said of John Chrysostom that it were better for the sun not to rise on Constantinople than for Chrysostom to stop preaching. Even in the dark Middle Ages, great preaching was not entirely lost. Bernard of Clairvaux was so persuasive in his sermons that it is reported mothers would lock their sons in the house to restrain them from following him back to the monastery. Francis of Assisi, though excelling in many Christian attributes, always considered himself first of all a preacher.[4]

When we enter the Reformation period, we observe preaching blossoming on a scale not known for many years. No one questions the fact that preaching was a vital and essential factor in the entire movement. Men like Luther, Calvin, and Knox were not only great theologians and writers; they were also very convincing preachers.

Had these men and their colleagues not been persuasive proclaimers of their doctrine, one wonders what would have become of the Protestant Reformation.

After the ministries of preachers like John Bunyan, the eighteenth century dawned and brought the advent of another era of great preaching. The names of men like Wesley, Whitefield, Edwards, Zinzendorf are still household words. As these men preached, spiritual awakenings occurred. The next century was little different except this was also a time of great pastoral preaching. Thousands flocked Sunday after Sunday to hear the oratory of pastors like Spurgeon, Dale, Clifford, Brooks, and Beecher. Simultaneously the revivalists were preaching to large crowds. Finney, Moody, Chapman, Torrey, and a host of others won thousands, even millions, to Christ. And where would the modern missionary movement be if it were not for the great preachers of the eighteenth and nineteenth centuries, men like Carey, Judson, Rice, Taylor, and their kin?

Even the twentieth century has not been bereft of effective preaching, despite the current downgrading of the practice. Billy Sunday, notwithstanding his weaknesses, is credited with winning a million people to faith in Christ. And no man in church history has preached to more people than our contemporary, Billy Graham. Moreover, there are men of God this very day who are filling their churches with worshipers who come to hear the Word of God preached.

In the light of a long and significant history, I make bold to conclude that the days of proclamation are not forever past. I am convinced a revival of effective preaching is not unthinkable at all. I believe evangelistic preaching can have a new day. I do not mean by this that we should retreat into the false security of living in the past. I certainly do not mean to imply we should disregard other modern methods of communication that technical progress has given us. I know a methodology can hold for centuries and suddenly, because of a radical change in circumstances, become totally irrelevant. For example, since matches have become available, few people rub sticks together to start a fire. And I am aware that some think preaching is like rubbing sticks. But I believe preaching can come alive in our day. Even in our empirical, existential, technological age, I feel preaching—yes, evangelistic preaching—can be very effective. As we develop our "go-structures," we can still find a very real place for the preaching of the gospel in the context of our church services. This I believe. It is not an either/or choice of our "going to them" or their "coming to us." It is developing every kind of evangelistic activity that I am calling for. But if we are to preach Christ effectively today, we must take a fresh look at the entire preaching enterprise.

Prerequisites of Effective Evangelistic Preaching

Three things seem absolutely necessary to communicative preaching today, especially evangelistic preaching. If preaching is to regain its historical role these principles are vital. First, there is the content of the proclamation. For evangelistic preaching to be successful, there must be a clear-cut positive presentation of the biblical meaning of the gospel. Second, effective methodology is essential. Here is where awareness to the preaching situation must be paramount. We must communicate to man in such a way that he will hear and act. The final consideration is the preacher himself. He must embody some qualities as God's man if he is to preach with effect. Preaching is always the communication of "divine truth through personality." [5] Let us look at these three principles in some detail.

The Content of Evangelistic Preaching

Although one never appreciates the type of preaching that grows out of a bigoted and narrow dogmatism, there must be no "uncertain sound" from the pulpit when the gospel is proclaimed. As Webster reminds us:

> A mood of uncertainty about the heart of the Gospel, the Lord of the Church, and the Savior of the world, is unworthy of Christians and bodes ill for the future of missions if it is allowed to be encouraged or persists. Describing the first mission to Thessalonica St. Paul wrote: "When we brought you the gospel, we brought it not in mere words but in the power of the Holy Spirit, and with strong conviction, as you know well" (1 Thess. 1:5, NEB). Christian, even theological, humility is not synonymous with vagueness.[6]

What then is our message? What is that "foolishness of the proclamation" (1 Cor. 1:21) that God uses to save men? This verse and the implication of Paul's statement to the Corinthians is a vitally important issue in regard to evangelistic preaching. We must look at it closely.

C. H. Dodd's Approach to the Kerygma

Ever since C. H. Dodd gave us his classic little volume *The Apostolic Preaching and Its Development,* much interest has centered on the idea conveyed by the New Testament word *kergyma.* Its importance is patent, for in the term we find the essence of the good news we are to preach. As Dodd approaches the subject, he makes a quite unbending distinction between *kerygma* and *didaskein. Didaskein* he defines as teaching, i.e. ethical and moral instructions on the Christian life. Occasionally, he tells us, it includes what we would today call apologetics. At other times *didaskein* contains theological doctrine, for example, in the Johannine writings. But *didaskein* is quite different from *kerygma. Kerygma* alone is preaching; preaching of the nature of a "public proclamation of Christianity to the non-Christian world." [7] Dodd concludes that much of the preaching in the contemporary church would not have been recognized by the early Christians as *kerygma.* What we hear in large measure on Sunday morning in many congregations is either teaching, exhortation (*paraklusis*), or a *homilia,* i.e. a discussion on the Christian life and thought directed to those who already believe.[8]

To preach in the New Testament sense of the word, Dodd contends, has for its object—at least the great bulk of the time—the gospel of Jesus Christ. He holds that the basic idea contained in the term *keryssein* is so close to that conveyed by the word *evangelizesthai* (to evangelize) that for all practical purposes the terms can be used synonymously.[9] He deduces:

> For the early church, then, to preach the Gospel was by no means the same thing as to deliver moral instruction or exhortation. While the church was concerned to hand on the teaching of the Lord, it was not by this that it made converts. It was by *kerygma,* says Paul, not by *didache,* that it pleased God to save men.[10]

What then is this primitive *kerygma?* What is the essence of our proclamation? Dodd's understanding of the essential *kerygma,* first in Paul's epistles, can be summarized in the following manner:

> The prophecies are fulfilled and the new age is inaugurated by the coming of Christ.
> He was born of the seed of David.
> He died according to the Scriptures, to deliver us out of the present evil age.
> He was buried.
> He rose on the third day according to the Scriptures.
> He is exalted at the right hand of God, as Son of God and Lord of quick and dead.
> He will come again as Judge and Savior of men.[11]

Dodd grants that the evangelistic preaching of Paul probably contained more than this, but it at least has the above if it can be called evangelistic proclamation at all.

Moving on to consider the preaching of Peter and the others as found in early Acts, Dodd discerns six basic elements in their *kerygma.* First, the age of fulfillment has dawned. The messianic age has come (Acts 2:16 ff.). Second, this new age has taken place through the ministry, death, and resurrection of Jesus Christ. And a brief account of this is always given. The concepts of the Davidic descent, the Lord's ministry, his vicarious death, and his glorious resurrection are presented. Moreover, these truths are presented in the context of scriptural prophecy fulfilled as determined by the foreknowledge of God. Third, by virtue of the resurrection, our Lord has been elevated to the right hand of God as messianic head of the "new Israel" (Acts 2:33-36). In the fourth place, the Holy Spirit is the sign of Christ's present power and glory (Acts 2:33). Fifth, the messianic age will reach its consummation in the return of Christ (Acts 3:21). And lastly, the *kerygma* in Acts always closes with an appeal for repentance, the offer of forgiveness, the gift of the Holy Spirit, and the assurance of salvation in the life of the "age to come" (Acts 2:38-39). Dodd then summarizes, "We may take it that this is what the author of Acts meant by 'preaching the kingdom of God.'" [12]

A contrast between the Pauline proclamation and the Jerusalem *kerygma* makes it clear that Paul emphasized three things that are not as explicit in the preaching found in the early chapters of Acts. One, in early Acts Jesus is not normally called the "Son of God." His titles are more in line with the prophecies of Isaiah. But Dodd states that the idea of Jesus as Son of God is deeply embodied in the Synoptic Gospels and these first three books of the New Testament were probably little influenced by Paul; the preachers of Acts were surely not averse to the idea of Jesus as Son of God. Two, the Jerusalem *kerygma* as over against Paul's preaching does little in declaring that Christ died for our sins. As Dodd puts it, "the result of the life, death, and resurrection of Christ is the forgiveness of sins, but the forgiveness is not specifically connected with his death." [13] Three, the Jerusalem *kerygma* does not emphatically assert that the ascended Lord intercedes for us as does Paul. As for the rest of the points in Paul's gospel, they are all found in the early sermons of Acts.

Michael Green and the Kerygma

Since the time Dodd wrote his classic, the bookshelves of pastors' studies have been filled with volumes that build upon his essential thesis. Wide and varied have been the approaches of these works.[14] Criticism of Dodd's ideas have naturally been raised. Recently, for example, Michael Green has contended that "there has been undue concentration on what has become technically known as the 'kerygma'." [15] He holds that Dodd and others may well have made the *kerygma* far too fixed. At one point he even raises the question as to whether or not there even was a fixed *kerygma.*[16] He argues that "the probabilities of the situation would militate against undue fixity in the presentation of the message." [17] What is to be grasped, Green argues, is that the background and understanding of the listeners helped determine what aspect of the truth of Christ was to be preached. Green is not alone in this contention. This is also the approach of Professor C. F. D. Moule in his book *The Birth of the New Testament.* Eduard Schweizer writes along similar lines in an essay found in *Current Issues in New Testament Interpretation.* Perhaps the best full-scale treatment of this problem is found in R. C. Worley's work *Preaching and Teaching in the Early Church.* It must be recognized, Green tells us;

> It would be a mistake to assume from studies such as those of Dodd that there was a crippling uniformity about the proclamation of Christian truth in antiquity, that there was a basic homogeneity in what was preached we may agree, but there was wide variety in the way it was presented. Nor was this variety always the result of the supposedly rigid and conflicting theologies which were prevalent in different sections of the ancient Church. . . .But much of the variety will have been necessitated by the needs and understanding of the hearers. Evangelism is never proclamation in a vacuum; but always to people, and the message must be given in terms that make sense to them.[18]

Still, Green grants, "there was a basic homogeneity in what was preached." What then is this "basic homogeneity" as Green sees it? He believes we shall not go far wrong in taking three basic points as essential to the Word the first-century church proclaimed.

First they preached a person. Their message was frankly and unapologetically Christocentric. This gospel message was not so much centered on his life and public ministry; rather, it was upon his death and glorious resurrection.

Green holds in the second place that the early church proclaimed a gift. It was the gift of forgiveness, the gift of the Holy Spirit, the gift of adoption and of reconciliation. That kind of grace made "no people" the "people of God." Concerning the idea of a gift, the emphasis was placed upon the gift of forgiveness and the gift of the Holy Spirit.

Third, the first-century church looked for a response from their hearers. The apostles were anything but shy in asking men to decide then and there for or against Christ. They expected results—positive results. These early preachers declared men must do three things in the light of the gospel.

1. They must repent. This was first and foremost.
2. They must exercise faith. A continuing life of faith was called for, but it must begin by a "leap of faith." True faith is inseparable from repentance.
3. The apostles preached baptism. It was seen as the seal on God's offer of forgiveness and the essence of man's response to that offer in repentance and faith.[19]

From this perspective, Green presents his understanding of the *kerygma*. And though there is probably validity in his criticisms of Dodd's more inflexible approach, it is clear he also sees the essential proclamation as a definable, propositional body of theological truth.

James Stewart and the Kerygma

Another interesting writer on the theme of proclamation is James Stewart in his popular book *A Faith to Proclaim*. In this helpful volume he tells us that the first axiom of evangelism is that the evangelist must be sure of his message. However, he does not, on his own admission, attempt to traverse again the ground that Dodd, Oscar Cullman, Rudolf Otto, and others have done in attempting to discover the primitive *kerygma*. His purpose is to find the bearing the *kerygma* has on present-day questions. So from this pragmatic perspective he gives us what he feels is that essential proclamation.

> What, then, was the essence of this proclamation by the original heralds of the faith? Quite briefly it was this. They proclaimed that prophecy was fulfilled; that in Jesus of Nazareth, in His words and deeds, His life and death and resurrection, the new age had arrived; that God had exalted Him, that He would come again as Judge, and that now was the day of salvation. This was the message.[20]

From the above statement Stewart derives five principles that should be found in all proclamation. To begin with, the evangelist must declare the incarnation. The facts of the *kerygma* are historical facts. The doctrine of the incarnation means that "God has come right into the midst of the tumult and the shouting of this world." [21] And the facts of the incarnation are not only historic, they are unique. The kingdom of God, no less, has broken into the here and now. That is unique and unrepeatable.

The evangelist also proclaims forgiveness. This is always very relevant, for "whenever the Church truly proclaims the forgiveness of sins there the healing ministry is veritably at work." [22] The feeling of meaninglessness in life so relative to our existentially-oriented society must be recognized as a problem of sin. Iniquity and rebellion against God are the ultimate culprits in the contemporary loss of identity and feeling of utter aloneness. As the church preaches forgiveness it strikes right at the heart of many present-day problems. As Kierkegaard said, "I must repent myself back into the family, into the clan, into the race, back to God." [23]

In the third place, Stewart states that the proclaimer preaches the cross. The veil has been rent; the veil which kept men out of God's presence and that which shut God in. The darkness and mystery of God's "wholly otherness" has now been flung open to men. Reality can be touched. As Stewart expresses it, "The death of Christ gives me the very heart of the eternal, because it is not words at all, not even sublime prophetic utterance: it is an act, God's act, against which I can batter all my doubts to pieces. We preach Christ crucified, God's truth revealed." [24] But the death of Christ does not stop at revelation. The apostolic *kerygma* goes much further. The cross speaks of atonement, guilt-bearing, expiation. Moreover, the demonic forces of the universe were once and for all defeated. Christ has overcome the world. "We preach Christ crucified" is always to be the cry of the evangelist.

Fourth, the "hour cometh, and now is." The new age, the long expected hope, has occurred. Christ has been raised. We preach a resurrected, living Lord. "This is indeed the very core of the apostolic *kerygma.*" [25] It was the theme of every Christian sermon. The fact of the resurrection was no mere appendix tacked on the end of their proclamation. The resurrection is a cosmic event. It is not just a personal victory for our Lord. All history was shattered by this creative act of God Almighty. The resurrection means that the whole world has died and a glorious rebirth has taken place. Nothing can ever be the same again. Naturally, the apostolic message did not see Good Friday and Easter as two isolated events. They were always presented as one mighty stroke of God. Now time has been baptized into eternity; things on this side immersed in things on the other. There is no atonement and reconciliation apart from the resurrection. It is God's act of justification. "This is our gospel. For this is what Christianity essentially is—a religion of Resurrection." [26]

Finally, and in summary, Stewart declares that the evangelist simply preaches Christ. The message is not a cold, conceptualized theology or philosophy. A person is preached. And what a person He is; the helper, shepherd, companion, friend, light and bread of life, our *paraclete.* If Christianity is anything it is an experience of a "vital relationship to a living Christ." [27] This is the great discovery the world needs to make. How different contemporary society would become if it truly understood what this means.

Stewart thus casts the *kerygma* in a pragmatic context. He applies all the essentials of the proclamation to living human situations. Surely this is what must be done in actual preaching. We must thoroughly understand our message theologically, but it must always be related in terms that addresses the *kerygma* to real life.

The Kerygma in Douglas Webster

Douglas Webster in *Yes to Mission* presents his grasp of the *kerygma* in four basic principles. He begins by reminding us that "mission implies that the Church does have something to say." [28] He states that evangelistic preaching must always center upon:

> 1. The person and character of Jesus Christ. He really did live and was unique above all other men.
> 2. The teaching of Jesus Christ. He said things about God, life, the Kingdom of God, and human destiny as no one had ever spoken before.
> 3. The death of Jesus Christ. The death of our Lord was the turning point in all history and God was ultimately active in it.
> 4. The resurrection of Jesus Christ. Death did not end it all for the Lord, rather it was the end of death, for He is a living Savior.

Webster correctly points out that though some want to add more to the gospel than the above four essential points, it is certain that "we cannot have less, if we are to retain the Gospel at all." [29]

Now what is to be learned from these and other varied approaches to the *kerygma?* Two lessons seem vital. To begin with, whether we take the more rigid view of men like Dodd or a more flexible approach like that of Green or Webster, there is still an essential and basic content to evangelistic proclamation if it is to be biblical in nature. There are certain theological and historical realities that must be clearly understood and declared in the presentation of the gospel. And it is clear that these basic truths center in and around the person and work of Jesus Christ. Second, and to our immediate concern about preaching, it must be stressed that our evangelistic messages must contain the essential *kerygma* if we are to expect God's full blessings upon our preaching. So many so-called evangelistic sermons today seem rather bereft of the real biblical content of the *kerygma.* Mere appeals to the imagination, emotions, or what have you are not what the New Testament understands by preaching. "We preach Christ"; this must be our theme in all our attempts to win men to Christ by preaching. I have a firm conviction that any preacher who aspires to preach the gospel *must be very careful* to have the essential content of the *kerygma* in all of his evangelistic messages. "Great gospel preaching," to use an old cliché, if it is true biblical gospel preaching, is filled with *kerygmatic* content.

The Methodology of Effective Proclamation

As important and fundamental as the content of preaching is, it is not the whole story of effective proclamation. The proper "preaching situation" is vital to the success of evangelistic declaration. What I mean by the preaching situation is the entire setting of what transpires in a meaningful evangelistic preaching experience. It must always be remembered that the activity of preaching is not merely a means for conveying the content of the Christian faith. Preaching is a unique activity in the Christian context. It is an event; an event wherein God meets man. It is a form of God addressing himself to man. As H. H. Farmer has put it:

> Preaching is telling me something. But it is not merely telling me something. It is God actively probing me, challenging my will, calling me for decision, offering one His succour, through the only medium which the nature of His purpose permits Him to use, the medium of a personal relationship. It is as though, to adopt the Apostle's words, "God did beseech me by you." It is God's "I—thou" relationship with me carried on your "I—thou" relationship with me, both together coming out of the heart of His saving purpose which is moving on through history to its consummation in His Kingdom.[30]

It is right here that the distinctive nature of effective evangelistic preaching appears. This is why preaching can be seen in one sense as a sacrament. Preaching is only distinctively Christian preaching insofar as it is both uttered and listened to in faith. In other words, baffling as it may seem, preaching is God's activity, i.e. it is God encountering men in the extreme and supreme crises of their lives.

Real preaching—*kerygma* or *didache*—depends upon the preacher conveying the sense of the living, saving activity of God in Christ.[31]

It should be said here that the distinction between *kerygma* and *didache* is not to imply that the two never blend. Nor should this distinction be understood as dictating methods of communication. The preacher in the pulpit can be in the context of *didache*. And a layman in dialogue with another can surely be in the spirit of proclamation. *Kerygma* is not to be understood as always a monologue, nor is *didache* always dialogue. What is to be sought is communicating the truth in the method that the immediate situation calls for. And as emphasized above, declaring God's word is always to be done in faith and heard in faith. This implies that all genuine Christian communication is something of a dialogue whether it be *kerygma* or *didache*.

These principles of Christian preaching indicate a number of things. Initially, preaching must always be viewed as a personal encounter. God confronts people in the preaching situation on a Person-to-person level. As Farmer expressed it, "God's 'I—thou' relationship with me is never apart from, is always in a measure carried by, my 'I—thou' relationship with my fellows." [32]

In this light one can see the position of the proclaimer. In the first place, he must be intimately related to God in an "I—Thou" sense. If he loses the reality of God's presence in his preaching, all is lost. He must also be related to his hearers in this "I—thou" manner of understanding relationships. The preacher stands, as it were, at the corner of a right-angled triangle. He is related vertically to God and horizontally to his hearers in the preaching situation. In the context of this setting God completes the triangle and confronts and addresses man. Moreover, there is give and take in all directions on the triangle. It is an existential encounter *par excellence*. As Miller puts it,

> The Romanist says, "When the priest pronounces the tremendous words of Consecration, he reaches up into the heavens, brings Christ

> down from his throne, and places him upon an altar to be offered up again as the victim for the sins of man." Protestantism, when it is true to its genius, does something better. When the Protestant preacher preaches—if he really preaches in the terms set forth here—the living Christ, who is always present in the fellowship of his people, both in heaven and on earth, expresses himself not in dumb symbol but in living reality, and offers once again to men the reconciliation with God once accomplished by His death and resurrection and now eternally available to all who will believe. Men do not see through superstitious imagination and as mute observers a magical transformation of material symbols by the official intervention of a priest. They are confronted by the living Christ himself, who chooses to make his eternal redemptive Deed effectual by making the word of the preacher become His own word in the fellowship of the members of His body.[33]

The immediate implication of this kind of preaching is that it is costly. Effective proclamation does not come easy. The preacher is giving of himself. The relationship is of an "I—thou" nature, not an "I—it." That always costs! The proclaimer is pouring out himself to God on the vertical dimension and pouring out himself on the horizontal to the people. He so gives of himself in the preaching experience that he is drained. Preaching can be painful when one gives of oneself as one ought. The pulpit is not a place to be cool and casual in spirit and attitude. It was Paul who said, "Therefore be alert, remembering that for three years I did not cease night or day to admonish everyone with tears" (Acts 20:31, RSV).

Finally, the preacher must keep people in his vision. As important as is the content of one's message, it is people that must be seen as central. We do not preach in a vacuum. We know, as already quoted from Stewart, that "the evangelist must be sure of his message." In this age of uncertainty and relativity this is more important than ever; but preaching is to people. It is to them we address our message in love, compassion, and understanding as we attempt to relate to them meaningfully. We speak to men in their life situation. Life situation preaching is a must these days. Thus, we conclude that all other aspects of methodology are secondary to the basic existential preaching situation we have described. This the preacher should understand and attempt to cultivate, for this is the context in which God works.

The Preacher Himself

A word about the man who declares God's message is in order. Dr. Raymond Brown reminds us that the effective preacher today must have three essential qualities.[34] He must first be an acute observer. It takes more than just understanding the Scriptures to be a preacher who is relevant to today's world. He must be a student of his contemporary society. He must know his world. The late D. T. Niles said, "If we want to talk with God we had better find out something about the world because that is the only subject in which God is interested." [35] The same surely is true if we want to speak for God. Roger Schutz has correctly confessed that often "we allow ourselves to be caught up in a Christian environment that we find congenial and in the process create a ghetto of like-minded people who are quite unmindful of the real world." [36] We must preach to real men in real life. But surely we have emphasized this principle enough.

The preacher must also be a compassionate listener. As Brown puts it, "Before he talks he must learn again to listen." [37] He must listen on a two-fold level; he must listen to God, and he must listen to people. He speaks for God to the needs of people. How can he effectively communicate unless he is genuinely open to both? We need to emulate the spirit of Ezekiel when he said, "I sat where they sat and remained there astonished among them." That was where the prophet learned to be God's spokesman.

And the preacher must be a discerning teacher. This we have already stressed in the previous chapter on the role of the pastor as one who builds up the church for mission. The need is obvious. If ever there was a day of alarming ignorance concerning the Word of God, this is that day. May God make of his spokesmen those who are faithfully "holding forth the word of life" (Phil. 2:16, KJV).

We can say by way of summary that the pastor-evangelist must simply be a man of God. He must be one who walks with God. He must know by experience—daily experience—the One for whom he speaks. As Farmer has well said, "I suppose in the end the secret lies in the quality of our own spiritual life and the extent to which we are ourselves walking humbly with God in Christ." [38] We shall have more to say about this in the last chapter.

As we now come to the final section on the theme of preaching the gospel, let us look into the actual evangelistic service itself.

The Evangelistic Service

Why is there a disillusionment among some today about conducting evangelistic services? Several misconceptions or problems seem responsible for tending to make our pulpit evangelism less effective, thus causing it to contribute to this disillusionment. Some pastors have been apparently hesitant in giving a whole service over to evangelism because of the relatively few unbelievers who normally attend. The obvious answer to this problem is that there are some there. And these, if only a few, need to hear the gospel preached. There also may well be more unbelievers attending than we realize. Just because practically all present are church members does not assure us all are truly regenerate believers. Billy Graham said that in America the greatest evangelistic opportunity is in the churches themselves. Furthermore, I believe that if pastors will faithfully develop good evangelistic services from time to time and forthrightly preach the gospel, the Holy Spirit will honor the effort and bring unbelievers along to hear the good news. I cannot even proof-text that statement, but experience and observation verify it for me. At this point, friendly, outreaching church members can greatly help the pastor.

A second problem is that some pastors tend to restrict their pulpit evangelism to just a short word of encouragement to accept Christ at the end of almost any kind of sermon or service. This practice is far from that which gets positive results. It is no substitute for evangelistic proclamation as we have attempted to define the idea. The whole service needs to be shaped and geared to the aim of winning people to Christ if it is to be decidedly effective.

Then, there are preachers who for one reason or another fail to give an effective challenge to the unbeliever. Consequently they see little result and are disillusioned with preaching evangelistically. This practice is to make the error of preaching only part of the *kerygma,* i.e. they may preach all about the Christ-Event but fail to remember that the apostolic message called men then and there to repent and believe. As John Stott has expressed it, "we must never make the proclamation without then issuing an appeal." [39] I have often wondered in the light of this principle why some pastors will not become exhorters and give a forthright challenge. Could it be because of the fear of failing to generate a response? Well, the response is not up to us. That is between the unbeliever and God. Ours is merely to challenge and help, theirs is to respond. Perhaps the reluctance simply grows out of timidity. But we are to be strong in the Lord. We have no reputation to keep or build as Christ's ambassadors. We simply do his bidding. We represent him. Of course, the type of invitation given should be of the nature that suits the situation. No one method suffices for all contexts. But surely the Holy Spirit can guide his ministers in how to do it. It is the failure to be guided that I think so often robs our pulpit evangelism of much power.

Probably the prime reason why some pastors view the evangelistic service as relatively ineffective today is because they feel inadequate and/or uninstructed on just how to develop a sound, sane, and spiritual evangelistic thrust in the context of a service. None of us feels expert in this. In such a high and holy venture, who does feel competent? But perhaps a few suggestions can help us all as we aspire to win men to Christ through preaching.

Simple Principles for the Evangelistic Service

Let the preacher first of all have confidence in the fact that, as George Sweazey states, "His pulpit still offers the minister his supreme evangelistic opportunity. No form of communication the Church has ever found compares with preaching." [40] Even if Sweazey has overstated the case, it is evident that the evangelistic preaching service has an important role in mission. Let us have assurance that God can and will use this methodology. If this be true, disciplines must be followed.

First and foremost, there should be adequate preparation. This must be seen in a two-fold sense. Initially, the minister must be fully prepared himself. This includes spiritual, mental, and emotional preparation. He will want to open the service not only with his sermon well in mind but with the assurance that it is the essence of the *kerygma* and that his basic objective is to win people to faith in Christ. He will also want to be prepared spiritually so that in faith he can fully expect God to bless the preaching of the gospel. This mental, spiritual, and emotional preparation does not come in a few moments. It is costly.

Preparation for an evangelistic service also means preparing the people as well as preparing oneself as the preacher. I think it a fine approach on occasion to inform the church in some fashion that an evangelistic service is planned for a certain date. Enlist the people to pray, to bring unbelieving friends, and then to come expecting God to bless and to draw people to himself. The more that is put into such a service, the more we have a right to expect God to honor it. Just to decide on Saturday, because a gospel sermon has not been preached lately, that Sunday is the time to preach evangelistically is a far cry from the kind of preparation needed.

Then it is vitally important that the proper atmosphere be developed in the actual service itself. We know this is essentially the work of the Holy Spirit, but there are a number of instrumental things God can use to create such an atmosphere. There should first be something contagiously dynamic about the entire service. There should be a positive spirit of joy. We are proclaiming the good news. The spirit of warmth, expectation, and joy that God's people exude is most helpful and provoking in itself. A number of things go into helping create this. Let me mention a few that may at first sound a bit negative. I think it is a time for relatively short prayers. There is, to be sure, a time for longer prayers, but the evangelistic service is not the time to pray for too many things. The unbeliever will not follow it. Long periods of announcements are not helpful. Further, the man who conducts the service should not be sombre and slow. The whole service should move along smoothly and rapidly.

Obviously, the right music is vital. Ideas concerning church music need a drastic updating in most of our congregations. The music in an evangelistic service can almost make or break its effectiveness. Edwin McNeely states: "It has been said many times that religion must 'sing or die,' for 'music . . . with its inherent emotional content, becomes a powerful force in drawing men into a proper relationship with God'." [41] The hymns chosen should present the gospel in a positive, enjoyable, and singable fashion. And let's be up-to-date in all selections, at least as much as possible. The time is overdue for hymns based on the language of an urbanized society rather than a rural nostalgia. Not too many people go to "The Little Brown Church in the Vale" anymore. One would hope that God would raise up hymn writers who can communicate the true message of Christ in the words and phrases that are meaningful to today's mentality and thought structures. Here is an area for much thought and prayer. I do not intend to imply that all the older hymns are passé. John Newton's "Amazing Grace" made the pop charts a few years ago. Be that as it may, an updating in most hymnology is urgently called for. Further, special music must be employed effectively. Choirs, soloists, groups, and instrumentalists should be employed skillfully. Parker said, "I believe that there is as much conviction lodged in the mind by singing as by preaching".[42] It is wise for the preacher to give serious, imaginative attention to the music phase of the service.

In developing an effective evangelistic service, little probably needs to be said about the actual preaching itself. This we have already discussed in some detail. The word of Blackwood concerning evangelistic preaching is enough here: "As for the preaching, every sermon ought to glow. It should be a burning message from the heart of God to the man in the pew." [43] But again, do let me emphasize the importance of extending an effective appeal. This must, of course, be guided by the Holy Spirit. He can lead and inspire his preacher what to do. Some years ago Faris D. Whitesell produced a book entitled *Sixty-Five Ways to Give Evangelistic Invitations*. He correctly makes the point in this book that the whole impact of evangelistic preaching "reaches a logical climax in the appeal." [44] Roy Fish has just produced a fine new book on *Giving a Good Invitation*. A preacher should not feel that he was born with the skill to invite others to follow Christ. It is something to be learned.

Finally, it is wise to involve lay people. Testimonies, special music, can often be used to project the idea that the service is really of and for the people. This obviously helps break down many barriers.

In a word, the preacher must be imaginative in creating an evangelistic service. When a creative, dynamic service is developed and the gospel is preached in the power of the Holy Spirit, I believe God will honor it. A short time ago I was conducting a service in a church in a very difficult situation by most standards. The entire hour was given to evangelism. The good news of Christ was presented in song, prayer, sermon, and spirit. After the sermon, I gave the appeal. God spoke, and people came to Christ. One of those who responded was a young man in his early twenties. His words to me were few but very profound. He simply said, "I want you to know I really met God in the service this morning." As long as that keeps happening, I for one will keep preaching the gospel and challenging people to come to Christ. As the poet Henry Crocker put it:

"Give us a watchword for this hour,
A thrilling word, a word of power,
A battle-cry, a flaming breath
That calls to conquest or to death.
A word to rouse the Church from rest
To heed her Master's high request.
The call is given, you hosts, arise,
Our watchword is evangelize."

Notes

1. Quoted in an unpublished address "Preaching Today" by Dr. Raymond Brown delivered at Spurgeon's College, London, 1969.
2. Ibid.
3. John Ker, *Lectures on the History of Preaching* (London: Hodder and Stoughton), p. 33.
4. Andrew W. Blackwood, *The Preparation of Sermons* (New York: Abingdon-Cokesbury Press, 1948), p. 15.
5. Ibid., p. 13.
6. Douglas Webster, *Yes to Mission* (London: S.C.M. Press Ltd., 1966), p. 20.
7. C. H. Dodd, *The Apostolic Preaching and Its Development* (London: Hodder and Stoughton, 1936), p. 7.
8. Ibid., p. 78.
9. Ibid., p. 8.
10. Ibid., p. 8.
11. Ibid., p. 17.
12. Ibid., p. 24.
13. Ibid., p. 25.
14. Michael Green, *Evangelism in the Early Church*, op. cit., p. 61.
15. Ibid., p. 48.
16. Ibid., p. 60.
17. Ibid., p. 61.
18. Ibid., p. 115.
19. Ibid., pp. 150-2.
20. James S. Stewart, *A Faith to Proclaim* (New York: Charles Scribner's Sons, 1953), pp. 14-15.
21. Ibid., p. 18.
22. Ibid., p. 50.
23. Ibid., p. 55.
24. Ibid., p. 82.
25. Ibid., p. 104.
26. Ibid., p. 110.
27. Ibid., p. 143.

28. Douglas Webster, op. cit., p. 18.
29. Ibid., p. 19.
30. Herbert H. Farmer, *The Servant of the Word* (London: Nesbit, 1941), pp. 27-8.
31. Ibid., p. 30.
32. Ibid., p. 56.
33. Donald G. Miller, *Fire in Thy Mouth* (New York: Abingdon Press, 1954), p. 34.
34. Raymond Brown, op. cit.
35. Ibid.
36. Ibid.
37. Ibid.
38. H. H. Farmer, op cit., p. 90.
39. John R. W. Stott, *The Preacher's Portrait* (London: Tyndale Press, 1961), p. 50.
40. George E. Sweazey, *Effective Evangelism: The Greatest Work in the World* (New York: Harper and Row, 1953), p. 159.
41. Edwin McNeely, *Evangelistic Music* (Fort Worth: Seminary Hill Press, 1959), pp. 4-5.
42. As quoted by Edwin McNeely, ibid., p. 3.
43. Andrew W. Blackwood, *Evangelism in the Home Church* (New York: Abingdon-Cokesbury Press, 1952), p. 129.
44. Faris D. Whitesell, *65 Ways to Give Evangelistic Invitations* (Grand Rapids: Zondervan, 1955), p. 11.

5 Obstacles to Effective Evangelism

It may appear slightly repetitive or perhaps even disproportionate to give an entire chapter to the obstacles a church faces as it engages in mission. Many of the current problems we face have already been mentioned. Yet it is surely appropriate to discuss in some detail certain paramount issues and then attack them positively in the hope that some guidelines to a solution can be found; effective evangelism may well hang on the issue.

The Modern Problem of Communication

Probably the most complex issue to be confronted is the modern problem of communication. I say "modern" because the problem is being felt today as never before in church history. Despite the complexity of the problem, the obstacle it presents to mission can be stated quite simply: how do we communicate the good news of Christ to large segments of society which virtually bypass the church as though it did not exist? In other words, how do we get the ear of modern, urbanized, technologically-oriented man?

But why, we are prone to ask, should the quandary of communication be such a stinging issue today? Do we not have means of communication at our disposal that the church has never had before? What has precipitated the situation? In answer to this basic question, it must first be understood that the essential nature of the problem is not as one would perhaps superficially suppose. What I mean is this: It is quite easy to see the issue as one of language, vocabulary, failure to use modern aids, and so on. These are problems, to be sure, but they are only secondary. Words and ideas are not the big hang-up in the communication tangle. The basic difficulty is essentially sociological. In recent years factors in the very fabric of society itself have so altered the fundamental nature of our Western sociological structures that communication has become an extremely difficult problem for all. Perhaps a cursory survey of the past few centuries will help us to see this in relief.

Ever since man has existed, he has lived in something of a tribal context. For millennia society was structured around a close-knit community in which man belonged. These communities were great sources of security because of their interdependent nature. The members of the tribe fished, hunted, worked, farmed together. Even their recreation was in a spirit of togetherness. One truly belonged. This community type of living provided man with a very viable society. With this kind of social structure, it is obvious that communication was no problem. As a matter of fact, tribal man could scarcely breathe without the whole community knowing and discussing it. His life was a shared life. He shared his ideas, his experiences, his very self with those of the community. He communicated with his fellows on a real depth level. This life-style was epitomized in the early days of our American frontier interdependent communities.

But approximately five hundred years ago—a very recent time in the light of man's complete history—a crack in the community dike appeared. The printing press came on the scene. The coming of the printed book began to change radically the entire structure of how the average man could receive information and knowledge. Before Gutenberg, only the elect few could have a library. Now all could potentially read. And how does a man normally read a book? Alone! Hence, we see the beginnings of the modern rise of individualism. The steps toward an "atomic" society began.

Then the industrial revolution began to break on the horizon in the Western world. This was more than a mere crack in the dike, a veritable tidal wave of social change swept across society and all but drowned community life as it had been known for ages.

Invention followed invention. Factories mushroomed to produce the fruits of the revolution. People moved by the millions from their old communities to the rapidly growing urban areas. Moreover, the new residential areas into which they moved were so diverse that their neighbors were not necessarily their fellow workers or hardly even acquaintances. To this were added long working hours and/or time-consuming travel. As the movement grew, isolationism deepened until consequently, as Gavin Reid states, "men have in fact become non-community animals." [1]

One further step was needed, however, to complete the breakdown of community. Many people still met in groups outside the workshop, for example, in clubs, hobby groups, the church. Then the technical revolution began to dawn and the step was taken. Television, radio, and the mass media put amusement and communication right into the home. Man no longer needed his social group. Leisure time could now be spent inside the four walls of his own castle—the home.

Thus, community broke down in the great urban crush of the exploding metropolitan areas. Of course, there are still the remnants of community here and there in the Western world. There are yet the small villages that have some form of communal life. There are also social and civic groups that center around some hobby or profession. But these tend to be very definite "in groups" with their own life-style and esoteric vocabulary. They normally consist of a quite narrow, restricted, peer group, and a ghetto mentality usually persists. Tragically, one can also view the church just like that. But the fact is that in America and western Europe over 80 percent of the population live in urbanized, industrialized areas where community to a certain extent has been obliterated. And if the prophetic sociologists are right, that number will go up to well over 90 percent in not too many years. In summary, we must just face the fact that community as man has known it for millennia is all but gone.

What does all this mean? It is simple: when community broke down, so did communication. Where there is no communal or tribal circle, how does one talk in depth to others? This is an acute problem for every facet of society. The businessman feels it; how can he get his product or service before people? The psychiatrist knows it only too well. Emotional illness due to isolation and failure to relate in depth to people is abounding. It is a desperate problem for the local church. If we cannot communicate to the masses, how do we get their attention to give them the good news of Jesus Christ? I hope we Christians can feel the depth of this disturbing issue. It is deadly serious for the contemporary local church. Actually, the church feels it more acutely than other aspects of society. The mentally ill either go or are sent to the psychiatrist. The businessman can solve his promotional problem by the use of mass communication. He can, for example, advertise on television or in the newspapers. But what about the average church? Society does not compel spiritually ill people to go to church. And in most of our churches it is almost impossible to get any kind of a foothold in the mass-media world; it is simply too expensive. Although this process is well advanced in Europe, it is a new but rapidly increasing problem in American society. It is already a different world in New York City as over against the tightly-knit communities of the "Bible Belt." And the urbanization mentality and its kindred problems of communication are creeping into the old bastions of Bible Belt life-styles also. For example, one of the highest crime rates in America is in Atlanta, Georgia.

Some have seen urbanization with the attending breakdown of community as a blessing. At last, they say, we can be alone and live our own lives without the gossip or interference of others. But the cost of this perverted kind of privacy is a high price to pay. With it we have lost a sense of belonging and with that the important feelings of security. Thus, we fail to communicate in any depth to our fellows except to a very few family members and close friends. It is right here where the church feels the crunch.

Where does all of this lead? To begin with, we must recognize that the church has a problem on its hands that it has never quite had before. As Reid points out, "It shows . . . that we do not start with the advantages of the Old Testament prophet, or of a New Testament apostle or even of a John Wesley. One thing was common to them all—they spoke to real communities and to community-man." [2] Today the urbanized church is not talking to men in community. It seems many Christians have not realized this fact. Our church programming is often still geared to people as if they were yet living in community with a tribal or rural mentality.

We must awaken to the seriousness of this issue. I think Reid is absolutely correct when he says:

> The greatest threat to the gospel today in our Western industrial societies is not communism, apathy, humanism, impurity of doctrine, or worldly compromise. It is this breakdown of communication not only from the Church to those outside, but also a breakdown of communications in every field of daily life. Unless Christians can find ways of saying things to modern non-community men then not only is modern man in a desperate plight, and not only is the Church facing extinction, but Almighty God Himself is gagged.[3]

Furthermore, the problem is probably going to get worse. The present-day metropolis is giving way to the huge megalopolis. Knowledgeable sociologists inform us that what remnants of community we have left will all but be swallowed up in the new gigantic area-cities that will stretch for hundreds of miles. Therefore, "We must not be surprised or downhearted if our towns and communities fail to show corporate responses to the gospel." [4] It will be logistically almost impossible for them to do so.

It is, therefore, quite clear that the old structures of church life that depended on speaking to men in community are over as far as their effectiveness is concerned. This, at least as I see it, is one of the big problems with our current local church life. This is one of the reasons I have advocated so strenuously the overhaul of many of our contemporary structures. We simply cannot continue to try to reach masses of urbanized people as if they were rural people—as they once were—and hope to reach them successfully.

A Suggested Solution

The whole problem for the church is obviously very complex and deep-seated. But perhaps the picture is not quite as dark as may at first appear. I think there is one thing the church can do that can be of real significance. If it has been the breakdown of community that has precipitated our failure in communications, why can we not simply recreate community? If we could do this, we could communicate the gospel in that recreated community. I think this is the principle we must grasp if we are to solve our thorny problem. I know we cannot recreate a social, tribal community as it once was. We cannot turn back the sociological clock. These great movements are beyond us.

What I mean is this: why not build little "communities" through the lives of the church members? Each Christian could become the center of a "mini-community," as it were. They already are in one sense. Everyone has his sphere of community, if it is only a few family members and friends. Why could not this circle become enlarged and developed into a sphere of Christian influence and Christian community? If members of the church could be enlightened to see this and then be led and equipped to build a community around themselves, here would be a tremendous outlet for communicating the gospel. After all, is not this the principle behind the house group, personal evangelism, youth Bible study groups, etc.? This is what we were trying to say in the concept of the lay-centered ministry. I think it is perhaps the most intelligent and relevant way to approach the ministry in the local church in our large urbanized areas—where most Americans live, or soon will.

Such an approach will mean that we cannot rely on what we do within the four walls of our church buildings to be the only or perhaps even our main evangelistic thrust. It also means we must release some of our overworked members from their million and one "church activities" so they can get on with building their "community" wherein they can communicate Christ. It further means that the church, the pastor in particular, must help to equip Christians for the task. We have already said much about this. But there it is: the breakdown in community and hence communication can be met by a new community through which Christ can be proclaimed. This, as I see it, is our hope for communicating the gospel today—and surely for tomorrow. Let's be prophetic and prepare for what is before us and not get caught with irrelevant methodologies for so long that we lose the ear of the masses. This is what has happened in western Europe. We must not let it happen elsewhere.

It may be helpful before moving on to other issues to say a few words about the secondary problems of communications mentioned earlier. There is the problem of language. The criticisms are quite true that with our inward-looking churches we have developed something of an "in-language." Our vocabularies must sound rather strange, if not unintelligible, to the modern, secularized outsider. It may well be that the "language of Zion" was once communicative to the man in the street, but that is certainly not the case today—especially to the younger generations. In reality, we are back to square 1 with the problem of the first-century church. They had to learn to use a common idiom to convey their message. So must we. But at least we are in good company as we attempt to face our difficulties.

To update our religious language is not easy, however. Old speech patterns and emotive words—emotive to us, that is—do not change easily. But we must attempt to proclaim the good news in a vocabulary that is understandable to the average man. It is true that we have many good theological words that are very descriptive. Moreover, a certain amount of technical terminology is inescapable in any field; look for example at the scientific world. Thus, the best course seems to be that we should use as simple a vocabulary as possible; then, when a more technical term must be employed that we think the outsider will not fully grasp, we should take ample time to define and explain and illustrate its meaning in words and pictures he will understand. This is what the apostles and early preachers did with the koine Greek. If we work at it, it is not difficult to communicate our message in terms that are understandable.

The point is that we become conscious of the problem and diligently work on it. For example, a short time back I had an opportunity to conduct a series of evangelistic services in Prague, Czechoslovakia. There were attenders who were completely outside the church. They lived in an utterly secular, atheistic society. The translator was not extremely fluent in English. Thus I had an external circumstance thrust on me that forced me to take the simple approach. I had to be very careful in the choice of many words, but by keeping in mind the centrality of communicating Christ and working with a simple vocabulary, I got the message to the people. Now if we can always see ourselves in a somewhat comparable situation, we should be able to declare Christ intelligibly to all hearers. And, incidentally, when we preach or speak, let us at all costs avoid that off-putting "ministerial" tone of voice. It may communicate all right but not what we desire.

There is another aspect of the problem of communication that needs serious attention: What is the source and meaning of truth? In chapter 1 we briefly discussed the issue. There we attempted to point out the spirit of relativism concerning truth that prevails in the thinking of modern man. All truth is somewhat relative, they would tell us. This way of thinking has to some extent influenced much of the younger generation. Subjectivism is the criterion of truth for many. Dogmatic pronouncements are frowned upon, especially when they come from those over forty. Not only that, empiricism and rationalism have all but won the day in our scientific and philosophical circles, not to speak of their influence on the man in the street. Consequently, spiritual concepts seem meaningless to many because they cannot be verified by sense perception. So when we talk about concepts that transcend rationalism, some people think us nonsensical. If we are not aware of this climate and move to meet it, many will reject our message which is by its very nature positive and spiritual and at times above mere rationalism.

There is an urgent need for an apologetic system and preaching that will meet the demands of this hour. Space forbids any such ambitious attempt here, but perhaps a few simple suggestions will afford some directions. Let us first recognize that any apologetic must be on a presuppositional level, i.e. we must "argue" from a presuppositional epistemological basis. Help can be found in the works of men like Francis Schaeffer, Bernard Ramm, C. A. Campbell, Rudolph Otto, and others. There are many good writings in this field. Let us remember we do not have to take an intellectual back seat because we believe the Bible to be the truth of God. And we must never forget that it is our responsibility to "always be prepared to make a defence to any one who calls you to account for the hope that is in you" (1 Pet. 3:15, RSV). Yet after all is said and done, it is the Spirit of God who convicts, convinces, and converts the unbeliever. As we positively present the *kerygma* without any dilution or shame, God will honor it. Moreover, it is often a moral problem more than an intellectual one that keeps people from Christ (John 3:20-21). Honest, intellectual difficulties can normally be met by the sincere and knowledgeable Christian.

The day also calls for a fresh look at the relevance of dialogue in communicating our faith. In Reuel L. Howe's significant work, *The Miracle of Dialogue*, he makes the point that dialogue is more than a mere method of communication, it is communication itself. It can develop depth relationships which are so vital to sharing one's faith. The wise minister will see that this principle is a real part of his life, service, and ministry. He will want to guide his people into the principles of dialogue. Is not this really at the heart of what we call personal evangelism? If Christians do not relate in depth to people, how can they win the unbeliever? Furthermore, church life itself should be structured in such a way as to allow for this type of interplay. People—at least young people—are moving away from a "come, sit, and listen" mentality. Many want to be heard. No longer can we ignore this growing sentiment if we want to communicate to today's world.

By the same token, the group method must be exploited for effective communication. A minister must learn the principles of group dynamics. But we have already said enough about that.

In the last place, concerning the problems of communication, it is surely wise to use all the modern means that are at our disposal. Audiovisual aids can be very helpfully employed. As much as one can move into mass media, radio, television, and print he should surely do so.

As fundamental and complex as the communication dilemma is, there is another very serious issue the church currently faces in its attempt to evangelize. We seem to be polarized between a "social action" approach to ministry and a purely evangelistic thrust. To this important problem we need to give a moment of attention.

The Problem of Social Action Versus "Frontier Pietism"

The conflict between what was once known as the social gospel and the advocates of evangelism pure and simple, "frontier pietism" as Gibson Winter calls it, is obviously nothing new. It has taken on quite a new complexion, however, in the advent of what is termed "secularization" theology. The old social gospel of a few decades ago has by and large given way to secularization thought. It is here where the battle shapes up today. These secular theologians are considerably diverse in their approach and in the depth of their radical orientation. John Macquarrie discerns three basic streams in this "New Theology." First, there is the school typified by Paul Van Buren in his book *The Secular Meaning of the Gospel*, in which he maintains that it is impossible to believe in any reality apart from that which is open to empirical investigation. For Van Buren, "secular" must be understood as excluding any kind of transcendent reality. It is obvious where this leaves traditional Christian theology. Quite correctly Macquarrie states;

> Thus Van Buren asked for what he called a "reduction" in Christian theology, so that its content might be brought entirely within the sphere of the secular. This "reduction" turns out to be a pretty severe mutilation of the traditional faith, for it means in effect that God Himself is to be left out. Van Buren's views are to be counted as belonging to the school that is trying to reconstruct Christianity without God.[5]

It is here that the radical death-of-God theologians find their home. Concerning this theological fad, which is thankfully quite passé now, no thinker equaled the excitement of Altizer. He alone raised the most fundamental problems for theology and the philosophy of religion. To a greater or lesser degree, other thinkers of the school like Van Buren are more or less traditional atheists. They can, thus, be dealt with philosophically on that level. But not so Altizer! He really believes that God once actually lived and then genuinely died. This is new. As Colin Lyas declares, "It is because Altizer means what he says to be taken literally that he is the really interesting and disturbing death of God theologian." [6] Again, lack of space precludes a discussion of Altizer's position, but an excellent examination is found in the cited article by Lyas.

Another approach to secular theology can be typified in Ronald G. Smith's work *Secular Christianity.* Smith's basic orientation is an existential understanding of history, i.e. he tends to follow the Bultmannian approach and interprets the New Testament in existential terms. Here we have a brand of secularity that lays stress on the temporal and historical but still attempts to retain the transcendent nature of God.

Finally, there is the sociological motif in the New Theology as seen in the well-known book of Harvey Cox, *The Secular City.* In this work, as Macquarrie points out, Cox "shows no special interest in either empiricism or existentialism . . . [but] lets his thought be guided by sociological rather than philosophical considerations." [7] Following Gogarten and others, Cox takes very seriously the secular mood of our time and regards secularization as the natural outgrowth of the Christian doctrine of creation. Cox holds that we are to look to God and cooperate with him in secular history and in the sociological structures and revolutions of our generation.

Within these three general categories most of the secularization thinkers rest. Perhaps it would be helpful to examine to some extent the basic ideas of one of these men who has been quite influential, Gibson Winter. Even though secularization theology is not the consuming discussion of the hour as it was a few years ago (process theology and the theology of hope are currently in the limelight), its influence is still very real and points up graphically the seeming conflict between social action and pietistic evangelism; hence our purpose in raising it here. A clear statement of Winter's position is found in his work *The New Creation as Metropolis.*

It must be understood that Winter and his colleagues are not anti-mission. The converse is much nearer to the truth—mission is central to their theology. The church must become the "servant Church," he tells us. "Amid the disunity and secularism of the city, the Church is the ministering servant of judgment and hope." [8] Moreover, the laity must be seen as the agents who are to fulfill the *missio Dei.* Winter says, "A laity, theologically self-conscious and socially alert, is the form through which the Church's witness in metropolitan society will be realized." [9] To this point one can find little disagreement with his principles. The rub comes, however, when we begin to discover what Winter means by mission. It is certainly not what we have traditionally understood as the evangelistic task. This is illustrated by his rather sharp criticism: "The piety of an individualistic frontier subverts the Gospel in an emerging metropolis." [10] He goes on to say, "Pietism replaces servanthood in the moment of metropolitan crises, disillusioning those who had looked to the churches for some direction in this hour of social class and racial conflict."[11] Thus, he clearly rejects pietistic theology, which has no doubt been a very basic influence in evangelism in the Western world for many years—and which, I would be prepared to argue, is essentially rooted in the Scriptures themselves. In Winter's rejection of pietism, it is not surprising to hear him speak of the Billy Graham crusades in these words:

> The crusades divert Christians from the real task of the Church in the metropolis. They distort the Gospel, the Church, and the character of the struggle to which the churches are summoned. The Graham crusade fosters pietism in place of servanthood. The Graham crusade uses the techniques of mass society to perpetuate the individualistic piety of the frontier.[12]

In the light of this quotation, it would not be very difficult to conclude what he would say about much of the evangelistic effort we see in evangelical circles today.

What then is "mission" according to Winter? In answer to this central query, Winter first makes a distinction between secularization and secularism. The differentiation is often made by this school. We have already seen this in Harvey Cox's approach discussed briefly in chapter 1. Secularism is idolatry, Winter tells us. It can be seen in all spheres; political, educational, even in the religious realm. In the religious life, secularism "is the substitution of religious structures and authorities for the Gospel."[13] We can see it, Winter contends, in the struggle between religion and evolution in the last century,[14] dogmatism about the Bible or particular "facts" recorded in biblical testimony,[15] dualism in the contemporary Church[16] and the current restriction of the religious life to the private sphere of the inner emotional life and intimate relationships.[17] Of course, some of these things most Christians would deplore. But two questions must be asked: (1) Does Winter think all evangelicals with a pietistic orientation are guilty of such an approach to the Christian faith? Surely he knows this is far from the case? Such a caricature is hardly fair. (2) Is the term "secularism" the best term to use for perversions of true Christianity? Why not use the simple old biblical word "worldliness," for that is what it is, and I see no reason why it is not still a good word to use as long as a definition is given. It surely communicates as well or better than "secularism."

But it is in the term "secularization" that Winter presents his whole idea concerning the *missio Dei*, and consequently that to which the Church must give itself. It is Winter's contention that what God is doing in the world is the bringing about of what he calls "metropolis." It is in this context, this "new situation," [18] that God's people are to find themselves involved because here is where God is involved. What is this metropolis that God is ushering in through the secularization process? Winter defines it in these words:

> Metropolis is the possibility of a unified, human society arising from the chaos of our massive, urbanized areas. . . . Metropolis is the realization of unity of life out of the conflicting factions which now plague metropolitan areas. Metropolis is the fulfillment of the oneness of mankind out of the division of races and classes that now disrupts the metropolitan areas of our country. Metropolis is the human society which different groups subvert and which all groups need for their well-being. Metropolis is the power of the New Mankind refracted through human history.[19]

Winter concludes, "To speak of metropolis, therefore, is to look with hope upon this metropolitan conflict; it is to see the Church in her vocation for humanity." [20]

This concept obviously implies a number of things. First, if God is at work essentially in the bringing about of a new unity and harmony in the urbanization process, he may very well be far more active in the office of Social Security than in the local church. Secondly, the church fulfills its primary role in engaging as a reconciling agent in this sociological process. Thirdly, the term "metropolis" is what we have traditionally meant by "the kingdom of God." Finally, the fact of the atonement must seemingly be understood in this sociological sense. This is obviously of profound significance. This certainly is a "new theology." This is quite different from the old social gospel. This is a radical theology indeed.

One may think that these theological speculations of the secularization thinkers are restricted to the academic ivory tower and are scarcely ever worked out in the heat of an actual mission situation.

This is not so. Many ministers seriously attempt to implement these principles into their understanding of outreach. For example, in a recent article an industrial chaplain laid out what he saw as the goal of his mission to men in industry. The secularization approach in the article was patent and his reliance on Gibson Winter admitted. The author's understanding of the aims of industrial mission read as follows:

> To be present in industry and to understand it.
> To stimulate responsible and critical thinking and to encourage and support those who carry responsibilities.
> To see the industrial situation in the light of a Christian understanding of things, and to do whatever may become possible there to help in the process of the word becoming flesh.
> To report back to the church, not only on what is happening out there, but also on the insights this work has found to be important.
> To set up the kind of flexible structure that will serve these objectives.[21]

He goes on to say that much traditional evangelism today is mainly born of "fear and despair" and is classified as "tub-thumping" and "bonhomie." [22]

There are several disturbing things about such an orientation to mission. But a positive word or two is in order. I think it applaudable that the secularization concept of mission sees man as a social creature and attempts to speak to him in that context. It is no doubt true that some current evangelism has been lacking in its realization of the fact that man is a gregarious creature. Perhaps individualism has been overstressed at the expense of communal concerns in some circles. Many evangelicals need to learn more profoundly the meaning of community needs. Moreover, it is important to know that God is at work in the great sociological movements of our time and that the full work of the Holy Spirit cannot be restricted to what he is doing in and through the instrumentality of the church. God *is* at work in the office of Social Security. Cox and others are quite right to take a fresh look at the doctrine of creation—evangelicals should as well.

But other questions arise—negative ones. Winter and his kin severely criticize those whom he sees as polarized on the individualistic aspects of the Christian experience. But after all, Jesus did come to save men individually as well as to redeem the whole creation, which travails until all is put right (Rom. 8:19-20). We shall do well to remember what Bryan Green tells us: "No task is more important or sacred than leading an individual soul into personal conversion." [23]

Why have Winter and these thinkers put themselves in this stance? They, too, are obviously polarized. Could it be because of what they understand by "metropolis"? This seems the crux of the matter. As already pointed out, Winter seems to equate metropolis with the kingdom of God. I suppose in one sense this is true; God is King over all. But Winter does not mean that.* He sees the emerging metropolis and all that it implies as the main work of God. It is here, apparently, that the atonement is essentially at work—not in the individual as traditional orthodoxy has always contended. Winter seems to be constantly implying that it is to straighten out the sociological tangle in the rapidly urbanizing world where the concept of reconciliation finds its primary meaning. This is what God is really doing. Or put it this way, individual conversion is out; communal or sociological conversion is in. And because this is what God is doing, this is where the church is to be involved. By ministering as the servant church to mitigate the problems of poverty, racial strife, class distinctions, ignorance and fear, and so on, we are fulfilling our basic mission. If he does not mean this, he should have made it clear.

What can we say to all this? Of initial concern, as important

*To be fair to Winter, it must be made clear that he does not equate metropolis with all that one finds in the metropolitan areas of the Western world. If I understand him properly, metropolis is an ordered, unified, harmonious entity within the city. And he sees it as emerging in the urban areas of the world.

and necessary and worthy as social work is for the church, Winter's theology seems to ignore totally all the Scriptures have to say about individual conversion. This we have already stressed. But it needs to be emphasized again that the New Testament is so clear and obvious on the point of the necessity of individual conversion that a defense seems hardly necessary. I realize this implies that I have presupposed the complete authority of the Scriptures. But I do make just such a presupposition. And I am convinced such a presupposition is far more defensible than that which the secularization men apparently take. (We *all* have our basic presuppositions.) Furthermore, quoting from my article written in reply to a paper on the aims of industrial mission,

> I am of the opinion that in the very depth of his personality, man is really asking, though usually quite unknown to himself, that old question of the Philippian jailer, "Sirs, what must I do to be saved?" Though he would rarely express it in these words today, the human heart still longs for God. After all, we are in His image and made for Him. And although a man may seek to fill the "God vacuum" in his life in a thousand different ways, he still longs implicitly to know the fellowship of his creator. This I firmly hold, on theological and practical psychological grounds. Thus when we answer man's deepest question on how to find meaning and reality in life through Christ, it is indeed good news that we share with him.[24]

Could it be that the basic error of Winter and others is that they are assuming a strange new brand of universalism concerning man's need of personal conversion? We grant that God is uniting all things. But the Scriptures make it clear that he is uniting things *in Christ* (Eph. 1:9-10). So if all men are somehow already in Christ, thus precluding the necessity of personal conversion, and the atonement is to be pragmatically seen as primarily applying to sociological structures, then Winter has a real point. In other words, if man does not need converting, and if what Christ did in the atonement is to be seen from the pragmatic perspective as essentially sociological, then by all means let us give our whole selves to the building of a grandiose brotherhood of men by social and political ministries, and it is all right if we call the product metropolis. But such a universalism is an assumption I cannot bring myself to embrace.

I have already admitted my presupposition concerning the authority of the New Testament, and I do not find in the Scriptures any theology of universalism. Therefore, I must reject secularization understandings of the *missio Dei.* I just cannot equate Winter's metropolis with what I grasp as the kingdom of God or the "New Jerusalem." Nor can I identify the "new mankind" of Winter with the "fellowship of the saints" that the New Testament presents. Citizenship in the new Jerusalem and a place among the fellowship of the redeemed comes through personal repentance toward God and faith in our Lord Jesus Christ (Acts 20:21). This is the basic truth—not the only one, but the basic one—the church is to proclaim and is, thus, the foundation of all evangelism.

Does this mean that God is not at work in the social structures of society? Again I emphatically say no! Of course God is at work in all that is for the good of man. This is the kind of God he is. And if God is involved in the sociological milieu of mankind, so must be his church. Let us do all we can to better the lot of our fellows. Let us work for all people regardless of who they are or what their need. This we must do if we are to be faithful to our Christian calling. But why be polarized on the meaning of ministry? Why let anyone, secularizationists or pietists, thrust us into an "either/or" situation? It is not either social action or individual conversion to which we are to give ourselves; it is both. So if a man is hungry, we feed him; if he is sick, we heal him; if he is oppressed, we unite to free him. I know also that we live in such a social structure today that, as Rutenber states, if we are to help the contemporary man who "falls among thieves" on today's Jericho Road, we shall probably have to form an action group and call ourselves the committee to make the Jericho Road a safe freeway. But by the same token, if a man is individually lost without Christ, we also meet that need by confronting him with the good news. If I give myself to some social need of man, I am not necessarily a "social gospeller," nor if I attempt to lead someone to faith in Christ am I necessarily a "tub-thumper" engaging in a gospel perversion called "frontier pietism."

What is so difficult about this relationship between declaring the gospel and social action? Why is the balance seemingly so difficult to keep? Why all of this polarization? The relationship between the two seems quite simple; we just find man where he is and in his need—whatever it may be, social, physical, mental, spiritual or what have you—and in the name of Christ we step in to meet that need. As James Leo Garrett has well said, "The crux of the present argument is that both evangelism and social involvement are essential to the mission and obedience of Christians today . . . the 'both/and' stance is to be taken rather than either of the 'either/or' stances." [25] I hope this is not oversimplifying that which is apparently a knotty problem for many. But in principle, I think it is that straightforward, and perhaps some have made more of a problem of it than it actually is. A well-rounded New Testament theology can surely motivate us to minister in God's purpose which is simply to find man in his multitude of needs and in the name of Christ meet those needs. And those who know their church history well understand how deeply involved the pietists were in social action. The great modern social movements grew out of pietistic evangelism. Gibson Winter should know that.

Now let us move on to consider an impediment to mission that is perhaps at least more keenly felt by the average pastor than any other obstacle.

The Problem of the Apathetic Church

A description of this obstacle to effective evangelism needs no elaboration. We know it only too well. Many church members are clearly "God's frozen people" to use the Gibbs and Morton title. How and when will the average Christian awake to his mission responsibility? It is even difficult to discern what has precipitated the growing spirit of lethargy. There are probably several reasons for the present spirit in many churches. There has been a lack of genuine worship with its vitalizing influences. The failure in rooting Christians in a knowledge of the Scriptures has no doubt contributed to a lackadaisical attitude toward the things of God. I have already attempted to make clear the importance of a local church understanding its role in the *missio Dei.* A lack of dynamic leadership training also has probably been a negative influence in some places. But regardless of these and many other possible reasons, one thing is certain, a spirit of apathy has settled upon many congregations that is profoundly serious. All ministers battle this problem to some extent.

What can be done to effect the spiritual awakening that we all desire to see so that the fires of evangelism may burn brightly? In principle, I think the answer is found in a word by C. William Fisher. He reminds us that "evangelism is really the outflow and the overflow of a spiritually vigorous church. Evangelism is the glow of an inner warmth, and the go of an inner compulsion. . . . Evangelism is not the cause but the result of a spiritual church." [26] If one agrees with the above statement, the issue ultimately becomes, how does a church become spiritually alive and healthy?

In answer to this foundational question, it must of course be said that this is God's work through the Holy Spirit. Therefore, to attack such a large theme in a few words is almost presumptuous. But perhaps a few things can be said merely by way of suggestion. The Holy Spirit uses means to effect a spiritual awakening, and if we can learn what some of these means are, we can make ourselves open to what he desires to accomplish.

In the first place, God has promised to bless and use the communication of his Word. But that teaching and preaching process must have certain ingredients. It must be prophetic, i.e. the Word of God must be positively and forthrightly declared with a relevance to human needs as they are today. We hear much emphasis on prophetic preaching, and rightly so, for "thus says the Lord" is what people desperately need to understand. The pastor should communicate the message with a relevant challenge. As I teach young preachers the rudiments of homiletics, I always strive to get them to see the necessity of a pointed object or aim in every sermon. A real part of that aim is to motivate people into action. This demands challenge. I am not asking merely for a "hard sell" approach. But I am saying we must "sell," no matter how we do it. We are to preach to move people to Christ. We preach for decisions. We need an element of exhortation. As James tells us, we are not to be mere hearers of the word, but also doers (Jas. 1:22). The preacher must always communicate the message with that principle and goal in mind. He *must* become a good expositor. What has happened to expository preaching? One rarely hears it anymore. We are to take seriously the call: "preach the word" (2 Tim. 4:2, RSV).

And when Christians discover their spiritual gift of ministry, they are usually strongly motivated. One time I was speaking on that theme when a dear lady interrupted me by blurting out, "I've got the gift of 'helps'." She was all aglow. It had just dawned on her what was happening in her Christian service. She almost jumped out of her seat as she related how God was using her. She was now aware of what was actually happening, and she was deeply moved. I saw her pastor a short time ago, and I asked how she was doing. He related that she was working harder than ever. It was a beautiful experience. When one discovers his real ministry, it has a motivating influence.

Further, the problem of apathy can perhaps be somewhat mitigated by attempting to correct those things I previously mentioned as some of the causes. We should strive to revitalize worship. We should keep the purpose and role of the church before our people. We should train the leadership. We must work towards making the local church a real "body of Christ." And as already stressed, we should do all we can to get Christians rooted and grounded in the Scriptures.

But I suppose that in the final analysis we are basically shut up to prayer and faith. If our churches are lethargic about the evangelistic task and in need of awakening, let us pray and trust God to revive his work in the midst of years (Hab. 3:2, RSV). That which we so desperately need, spiritual awakening, comes essentially through prayer. We who are leaders in the church may need to pray first for ourselves that the quickening may begin in us. When our own hearts burn, let us start working with those of like spirit. It may be only one or two at the start, but that kind of fire God can spread. I feel we have made a mistake oftentimes in attempting to involve the whole church in everything. It may be a very small remnant through whom God will send his blessings. Let us work and pray with those who are open for all that God has, and trust him to open up other lives as well.

These suggestions do not seem very exhaustive to meet such a pressing issue as apathy, but to be frank, I do not know of any shortcut to spiritual renewal. Yet, the signs seem to be multiplying that God is at work in marvelous ways among his people. We can and should take courage in the Lord. Renewal may be on its way.

We now move to the final problem to be discussed.

Conserving the Results

Every pastor has experienced the disappointment of seeing a person make a profession of faith, carry on for a time, and then seemingly fall away. How do we meet this situation and conserve the results of our evangelistic endeavors? May I present a few simple guidelines!

Initially, there must be a proper presentation of the gospel itself. That goes without saying. We must be careful to avoid ministering in such a way that our new converts stand in man's wisdom rather than in the power of God (1 Cor. 2:5). But given that, a proper philosophy of new member orientation is then called for. Often in classes or groups where new inquirers are taught, a basic mistake is made. It seems at times that new converts are given far more instruction on how to be a good church member than on how to be a good Christian. That is, more effort is spent on integrating them into the structures of the local church than into the basics of spiritual growth. As important for Christian maturity as the local church is, the prime need of the new convert is to learn the great disciplines and doctrines of the Christian experience.

There are at least seven points, it seems to me, that should form the foundation of new Christian orientation:

1. A rooting and grounding in the salvation experience. The new convert must know he is in Christ and secure.
2. An overall grasp of the great doctrines of the faith. Such a basic orientation seems essential for his understanding of all that transpires in his developing Christian experience.
3. An understanding of what the Bible is and how to read it profitably. The new babe in Christ is to desire the sincere milk of the word that he may grow thereby. (1 Pet. 2:2).
4. A basic primer on prayer. If one is to be strong in Christ, one must learn how to pray.
5. A grasp of how to achieve victory in trials, temptations, and testings. In Christ there is victory and the new Christian must learn how to be an overcomer.
6. The meaning and place of the local church in one's life. This is obviously a very important part of orientation into Christianity.
7. The necessity of witnessing and service. The new Christian needs to understand how to begin a life of witness and service for Christ.

If a new convert and church member gets established in these seven areas, he surely stands a far better chance of carrying on in his Christian life. If proper materials to teach the above principles are unobtainable, let the pastor write and produce his own.

Another profitable program that many churches have used with success is the assignment of "shepherds" to the new members. Let one or more be responsible for the nurture, care, and guarding of the young "sheep." These so-called shepherds must obviously be mature themselves and will need to be trained for the task. Some administration for such a program is also called for, but the results are well worth the time and effort.

Finally, the pastor himself will do all in his power to be a guardian of the whole flock—particularly the new sheep. Every minister knows his responsibility here, and the imaginative pastor can find a myriad of ways to help the new convert grow.

There are problems that impede evangelism to be sure. Many we have not even touched upon. But the pastor and Christian worker must remember that no problem is greater than God. If God is in this mission enterprise we have been talking about, solutions and success can be found. The pastor has fabulous resources to be a victor in this battle. It is to a consideration of these resources we now turn in the final chapter.

Notes

1. Gavin Reid, *The Gagging of God* (London: Hodder and Stoughton, 1969), pp. 20-21.
2. Ibid., p. 22.
3. Ibid., p. 17.
4. Ibid., p. 23.
5. John Macquarrie, *God and Secularity* (Philadelphia: Westminster Press, 1967), pp. 21-2.
6. Colin Lyas, "On the Coherence of Christian Atheism" from *Philosophy*, January 1970, vol. XLV, No. 171, p. 8.
7. John Macquarrie, op. cit., p. 25.
8. Gibson Winter, *The New Creation as Metropolis* (New York: The Macmillan Company, 1963), p. 54.
9. Ibid., p. 11.
10. Ibid., p. 25.
11. Ibid., p. 18.
12. Ibid., p. 17.
13. Ibid., p. 43.
14. Ibid., p. 44.
15. Ibid., p. 45.
16. Ibid., p. 46.
17. Ibid., p. 47.
18. Ibid., p. 2.
19. Ibid., pp. 2-3.
20. Ibid., p. 5.
21. R. P. Taylor, "Industrial Mission" from the *Baptist Quarterly*, January 1969, vol. XXIII, No. 1, p. 13.
22. Ibid., p. 1.
23. Bryan Green, *The Practice of Evangelism* (London: Hodder and Stoughton, 1951), p. 149.

24. Lewis A. Drummond, "What Is the Goal of Industrial Mission," from *The Baptist Quarterly,* July 1969, vol. XXIII, No. 3, p. 109.
25. James Leo Garrett, Jr., "Evangelism and Social Involvement," from *Southwestern Journal of Theology,* Spring 1970, vol. XII, No. 2, p. 60.
26. C. William Fisher, *The Time Is Now* (Kansas City: Beacon Hill Press, 1950), p. 69.

6 The Resources and Power for Effective Evangelism

This final brief chapter serves as something of an epilogue to our appeal for evangelism. In these closing pages I want us to see that there is power to be successful in mission. Resources are available upon which the pastor-evangelist or any Christian can call that will enable him to make a significant impact for Christ and his gospel. And simply put, that is what the *missio Dei* is all about.

The Power of a Holy Life

When one's service and ministry are finally summed up, that which makes the most lasting and vital impression is a Christlike life. As a young minister I once had the opportunity of serving as associate pastor to a true "man of God"—and I do not use that term lightly. This man was not the pastor of a large, influential church. He was not an outstanding or eloquent preacher. His intellectual achievements were not extraordinary. Yet his ministry was felt over a large area. Many came to faith in Christ through his witness. The one fact of his ministry that was so outstanding and that which gave him such influence was the profound godliness of his life. Although he passed on some years ago, the man's impact still remains. This implies a number of things.

In the first place, the image of the pastor-evangelist is extremely relevant to the effectiveness of his ministry. As Gavin Reid pointed out in his work on Christian communication, "Image communication can have an important supporting role to play." [1] This is true for any Christian, pastor or layman. Recognizing this important principle Paul said, "Brethren, join in imitating me, and mark those who so live as you have an example in us" (Phil. 3:17, RSV). When a man can honestly make such a statement, his life will prove powerful in mission.

Further, one's native ability is not necessarily the determining factor in an effective evangelistic ministry. It is obvious that God uses our talents, but as long as one's life is totally committed to Christ, God will make that life useful in mission—one talent or ten. And remember, he gives everyone "gifts" to serve him.

It is important, therefore, for all who aspire to be instrumental in evangelism to learn the principles of godly living. These principles are few and elemental. The entire concept can be summarized as simply knowing God in the experiential fellowship of Jesus Christ. As John in his first epistle puts it:

> That which was from the beginning, which we have heard, which we have seen with our eyes, which we have looked upon and touched with our hands, concerning the word of life—the life was made manifest, and we saw it, and testify to it, and proclaim to you the eternal life which was with the Father and was made manifest to us—that which we have seen and heard we proclaim also to you, so that you may have fellowship with us; and our fellowship is with the Father and with his Son Jesus Christ. And we are writing this that our joy may be complete. This is the message we have heard from him and proclaim to you, that God is light and in him is no darkness at all. . . . if we walk in the light, as he is in the light, we have fellowship with one another, and the blood of Jesus his Son cleanses us from all sin (1 John 1:1-5,7).

It is clear from this passage that daily fellowship with Christ—walking in the light as he is in the light—is the essence of knowing God. Perhaps this foundational idea can be illustrated in an experience of a young minister who, as the story goes, had much admired the ministry of an aged man of God who was to bring an address in his city. The young minister, thinking that perhaps he could discover some secret that would unravel the mystery of the tremendous success of the old minister, went to the service seeking that which would give him the insight to a similarly effective ministry.

When the time of the service arrived, however, the old preacher, though present, was not well and it was impossible for him to deliver his message. The convener of the meeting prevailed upon the elderly gentleman to say just a word. As the old servant came to the podium it seemed as though the presence of Christ settled down on the entire congregation. He then made one simple statement. He said, "I'm glad that I know God." These words fell like a hammer on the young minister. "That's it," he exclaimed to himself, "that's his secret. This man truly knows God." Most would agree that the young minister made a correct analysis of the situation. If our lives are to be effective and successful as God counts success, if we are to make the impact upon our communities and our world that God intends for us to make, if we are to experience genuine renewal in our lives and in our churches, we must come into a living knowledge and true fellowship with God himself. In a word, we must come to know God, vitally and dynamically.

Several things need to be said concerning the possibility of knowing God in the sense of living daily in his presence. Initially, it needs to be understood that as John saw it, Christianity was neither a speculative system of thought nor simply a mystical existential experience. It was a mysticism of genuine communion with God as revealed objectively in his Son Jesus Christ.

John also views fellowship with God as a marvel. It is marvelous because of the fact that "God is light and in him is no darkness at all" (v. 5). The metaphor concerning the character of God as "light" is used in various places in the New Testament. This figure of light obviously refers to God's holiness, and from the various New Testament passages where this picture is drawn we can grasp something of the marvel of what it means to walk with God in the light. First, God is complete light. John put it this way: "In him is no darkness at all." God is completely and unequivocally morally perfect. His righteousness is infinite and ultimate. He is absolute holiness. God is light—complete light—and in him is no darkness at all.

Not only is the light that surrounds the Godhead infinite and ultimate, it is also unchangeable light. James wrote, "Every good endowment and every perfect gift is from above, coming down from the Father of lights with whom there is no variation or shadow due to change" (Jas. 1:17). How different we are. We change; the moral and spiritual tone of our personalities can go from the heights to the depths. But God's holiness is utterly unchanging. He can always be experienced as "the same yesterday, today and for ever" (Heb. 13:8). He is always perfect, unchangeable light.

Paul states on the same theme in 1 Timothy 6:15-16 that God's holiness is unapproachable light: "The King of kings and Lord of lords . . . alone has immortality and dwells in unapproachable light, whom no man has ever seen or can see. To him be honor and eternal dominion. Amen." A new appreciation of the holiness, sovereignty, and majesty of the God of light is a needed contemporary concept. The current humanistic overtones about God as "the man upstairs" or the sentimentalism that states "somebody up there likes you" brings the God of holiness down to a level that is not found in the Scriptures. A fresh vision of the glory of God like that which Ezekiel received—even in Chaldea where one would not expect it—is a real need, for when the prophet saw God for who he actually was, he fell on his face in the dust (Ezek. 1:28). We must never forget that God is light and his holiness is utterly unapproachable by sinful man in the flesh. Though he is intimate and concerned for us all, he is absolutely holy.

This is what makes the possibility of fellowship with God the wonder it is. God is light, and we are darkness, the very antithesis of light. We hardly need be reminded that we are often found walking in sin's darkness. Nevertheless, we can actually walk in the light.

That is a marvel. How can it be?

Fellowship Through Confession

Fellowship with God is a glorious possibility. A holy life is conceivable. Yet it must obviously be worked out in the practical sphere of everyday living if it is to have any dynamic in one's experience. Foundational to the pragmatic implementation of the experience is the realization that fellowship begins with confession. John tells us:

> If we say we have fellowship with him while we walk in darkness, we lie and do not live according to the truth; but if we walk in the light, as he is in the light, we have fellowship with one another, and the blood of Jesus his Son cleanses us from all sin. If we say we have no sin, we deceive ourselves, and the truth is not in us. If we confess our sins, he is faithful and just, and will forgive our sins and cleanse us from all unrighteousness (1 John 1:6-9).

From the historical perspective, as we know, John was dealing with the error of the Gnostic concept that human flesh was sinful in itself. The Gnostics further erroneously taught that because God is spiritual and holy and because the human body is corrupt, the two could never meet. This brought them into very heretical ideas concerning the person of Christ and to grave moral errors concerning their own conduct. First, they could not conceive that Christ came in the flesh. Second, they felt that as long as the flesh was sinful and God was interested only in the spirit, moral laxity was permissible. All manner of sin was thus condoned. Now gnosticism as a system has passed away, but the sin issue surely has not. To us, even as Christians, sin is an ever-present quandary. And if we do not learn how to deal with sin as it invades our experience, we will discover that vital fellowship with God is just as unreal a dream for us as it was for the Gnostics. We must never forget that God is light and cannot sanction sin.

How are we to deal with this problem of sin? This is the basic issue, for this alone is what disrupts communion with God. The fundamental truth is in verse 7: "If we walk in the light, as he is in the light, we have fellowship with one another, and the blood of Jesus his Son cleanses us from all sin." The key phrase in the verse is the final statement where John says the blood of Jesus, God's Son, continually cleanses us Christians from all sin. (That is the force of the verbal tense John uses.) This simply means that if we are to walk in the light, we must constantly be cleansed by the power of Christ's forgiveness. Could it be that our proclamation of the death of Christ as the remedy for the sinful life has been restricted too much to our historical past, to the time when we first trusted Christ? John is telling us that Christians are to be constantly, daily cleansed by the blood of Christ. The death of Christ was not efficacious only on the day of conversion. His sacrifice is to be effectual in forgiveness every day. It is sanctification, not justification, that John is speaking of. But Christians must learn the importance of this work of God in their experience and recognize the centrality of the daily cleansing from sin by Christ. It is not going outside scriptural emphasis at all to say that walking with God can only be realized in the context of constant, daily cleansing from our sins by the power and forgiveness of Jesus Christ. This is what dispels our darkness so we can walk in the light.

I imagine that much of what has been said to this point will find a reasonably ready acceptance by most. Yet it is right here that nebulous thinking begins to creep in. The bulk of us would probably agree we need daily cleansing. It seems, however, that too few have actually grasped the biblical concept of how the believer is to deal with his sin in order that the blood of Christ may be efficacious in cleansing him and thus keep him in fellowship with God. This idea must be investigated in a little more depth.

The first step in experiencing the cleansing of one's sins centers in a proper understanding and evaluation of how sin manifests itself in life's basic relationships. It must be seen that sin usually presents itself in one of three ways. First of all, there is sin that involves the Christian and his relationship to God alone. Then, there is sin that involves not only the Christian and God but also one's relationship to another individual. Although every sin is basically and essentially an affront to God, at times other individuals are involved.

Third, there is sin which involves the Christian as an individual in relationship with God and also a group of people like the church.

When Christians see their daily sins as a nebulous, indefinite whole, they are not moved to deal with them in God's prescribed manner. We must see our sins specifically and individually, and to a greater or lesser degree we should categorize them as pointed out above. This is very important. As sin is seen in sort of a category, then it can be dealt with accordingly—and scripturally, for the Bible deals with them on such a basis. Let us see how this works.

Take the problem of sin as it involves just the believer and his personal relationship with God. What does the Bible say concerning this issue? The answer is found in 1 John 1:9, "If we confess our sins, he is faithful and just, and will forgive our sins and cleanse us from all unrighteousness." The word "confess" is obviously the key term in this verse. In the language of the New Testament it is a most interesting word. It is a compound word, comprised of the verb "to say" and the adjective "the same." This implies that to confess sins is "to say the same as" or "to assent to" the convicting Spirit of God that the particular thing in one's life of which the Spirit of God is convicting one actually is a sin. It must be recognized that the Spirit of God always deals with specifics in the Christian's life, not with sin as a principle. That aspect of the problem for Christians was settled on the day of conversion. In other words, to confess sins scripturally is "to concede to" or "to agree with" the voice of God as he convicts us of some particular act of rebellion that it truly is a sin. This precludes that which we perhaps could call a "blanket" confession of sins. For example, how often do we pray and hear other people pray, "Lord, forgive me of all my sins!" Such a prayer may be acceptable for public worship, but this is not the way the Scriptures state a Christian is to confess privately and fully. To confess sins according to 1 John is to name them individually, one by one, agreeing with the Spirit of God that the particular act of which he convicts one is a sin. As Christians we do not commit our sins as a big nebulous whole; they are individual acts of rebellion.

The confession of our sins should not be in a general indefinable manner either. They should be confessed individually. This is why we must see them individually. This clearly implies we must stay before God and walk in his presence and permit the Holy Spirit to search us out, convict us, and place his finger on those particular deeds that constitute our sins. But having then acknowledged them before God in this prescribed manner, we have the assurance that the blood of Jesus cleanses them.

Perhaps it will be helpful to recount a personal experience here. Miss Bertha Smith, a retired missionary, spoke in our church one time. Her message was along the line of confession, and she urged us all to write what she called a "sin account." She instructed us to take a piece of paper and on the left-hand column write down several numbers, and then in the quiet of a secret place before God, pray that the Holy Spirit would reveal every single thing in one's life that was displeasing to him, that had grieved him, and that had marred our fellowship with him. As a Christian I wanted to be led into all that God had for me; so I took Miss Smith seriously. I did that which she had urged us to do; I made out my personal "sin account." Much to my humbling, the Spirit of God brought unconfessed things to my mind that I had committed months, even years ago. I wrote them down. Then one by one I brought them back before God and confessed them by acknowledging with the convicting Holy Spirit that those things were actually sins of which I was guilty. When I confessed them like this, how precious the blood of Christ became.

This was not a time of morbid, neurotic introspection such as some seem to enjoy. It was not anything like that at all. This we must never permit ourselves to do. It was simply an honest evaluation of myself before God. Thus it brought a great release, not depression.

It was one of the most liberating experiences of my Christian walk. A new fellowship with God was experienced.

But as we have seen, some of our sins may manifest themselves in relation to others as well as to God. In such an instance to confess these sins to God alone is insufficient to experience the full release of Christ's forgiveness. To be sure we should confess them to God. But Jesus further stated in the Sermon on the Mount that if we have sinned against another and at the same time "are offering your gift on the altar, and there remember that your brother has something against you, leave your gift on the altar and go; first be reconciled to your brother, and then come and offer your gift" (Matt. 5:23-24). I do not think we can avoid the simple truth presented here. If we sin against another person and our fellowship is thus marred, restitution must be made to that person as well as to God. In the light of Jesus' statement, it is surely implied that to fail to acknowledge sins against individuals and *to* those individuals (as much as is possible under present circumstances and as God leads), we cannot expect deep fellowship with God or one another. I shall never forget the first time this truth came home to me. This was several years ago while I was pastor of a small church in Fort Worth, Texas. A young, deeply spiritual man preached on this theme in our church, and the Spirit of God bore witness to this truth to all of us. Many of us were compelled by the Spirit to put things right with different people.

Again let it be clear that I am not speaking of a morbid introspective seeking and digging out of past sins in one's life. Still I am thoroughly convinced that the Spirit of God is grieved over unconfessed, unforsaken sin. God is light, and we must take our darkness seriously. We must come to grips with ourselves as we truly are if we are to have the fullness of fellowship with God.

The seeking of forgiveness by those against whom we have sinned is certainly fundamental in our walking in fellowship with one another. Not only does it get our lives right with God, but also it keeps us right with one another. After all, it is the only honest, ethical thing to do. If God expects us to confess our sins to him to have fellowship with him, certainly the principle applies to our human interpersonal relationships. If there could be something of a real openness among ourselves, if we could embrace one another in the arms of confession in the context of a true binding of our lives in love and forgiveness, our homes, our churches, and our nation could be revolutionized. If fellowship with God and with one another means anything, it surely means this.

Finally, we found that sin at times has some relation to a group. It may be we have a particular problem, secret or otherwise, that others could help us with; or it may even be open sin that a whole group is knowledgeable of. How is this issue to be dealt with? James tells us, "Confess your sins to one another, and pray for one another, that ye may be healed" (Jas. 5:16). Does this mean that we are to confess our faults openly one to another? Does James mean to imply that there are times when we should confess some of our sins to someone or perhaps even to a group in the church as well as to God? This seems to be his meaning. There should be some person or group in the fellowship of believers to whom we can be quite open, honest, and candid about ourselves. Is not this really what the true "fellowship of kindred minds" means? Is not this the *koinonia* of love the New Testament talks about? The church should be such a fellowship of love and understanding that we feel unthreatened in opening our real selves to our brothers in Christ.

But let us be most careful here. This is not to degenerate into an open airing of our "dirty linen" to the whole world. Some have fallen into this trap. I should suppose that there are some areas of our lives that only God should ever know. At the same time, however, there is a need of genuine openness among God's people. We should drop the mask we tend to hide behind. As sensitivity to the Holy Spirit is developed and the fellowship of believers deepens, he will surely open the door so that it will be clear what should be shared and with whom. One would hope all our churches could grow into such a fellowship of love, understanding, and healing. Of course, if one's sins are so gross and well-known that reproach is brought upon the entire church and the fellowship of the church broken thereby, then forgiveness should obviously be sought from the entire church. This is what lies behind the principle of church discipline that many congregations have apparently forgotten today. And this I should imagine is what a public rededication of one's Christian life should really involve.

Now all of this must be seen in the most positive light. For when it is sanely, maturely, and scripturally approached, it is found to be a most liberating experience. When we become open with God and others, we can become our real selves. There has never been a deep spiritual awakening where this has not taken place. This is real fellowship with Christ and the essence of Christian community.

Victory over Temptation

It is hoped that all that has been said to this point concerning sin and confession will not leave the impression that in Christ there is no victory over daily temptations and that our experience of God is nothing more than a continuing cycle of temptation, sin, confession, forgiveness. The Scriptures are quite clear that God gives power over temptation as we walk in fellowship with him.

> Thanks be to God, who in Christ always leads us in triumph (2 Cor. 2:14).
>
> The law of the Spirit of life in Christ Jesus has set me free from the law of sin and death (Rom. 8:2).
>
> In all these things we are more than conquerors through him who loved us (Rom. 8:37).

The only conclusion that can be drawn legitimately from these verses is that in Christ there is victory over daily sin. But the issue is, how can that victory be achieved? We have surely learned that in our own strength we are powerless against some, if not many, temptations. What is the answer? It is important we find out; the practical holiness of our life is obviously quite dependent upon it.

The Way of Victory

John also deals with this issue in his first epistle. He tells us, "This is the victory that overcomes the world, our faith" (1 John 5:4). John says the way of victory is the way of faith. It surely does not lie in our own self-effort or self-determination no matter how we may strive (Rom. 7:18). Victory comes only through faith. Paul presents the same idea when he states, "above all taking the shield of faith, with which you can quench all the flaming darts of the evil one" (Eph. 6:16). Faith is the victory!

But faith must have an object. It will not do simply to say, "Have faith!" Genuine faith always has its foundation in truth. So it is in the matter of victory over sin. In what reality then are we to place our faith? It is to be centered in the truth that Romans 6:1-14 presents:

> What shall we say then? Are we to continue in sin that grace may abound? By no means! How can we who died to sin still live in it? Do you not know that all of us who have been baptized into Christ Jesus were baptized into his death? We were buried therefore with him by baptism into death, so that as Christ was raised from the dead by the glory of the Father, we too might walk in newness of life. . . .
>
> We know that our old self was crucified with him so that the sinful body might be destroyed, and we might no longer be enslaved to sin. For he who has died is freed from sin. But if we have died with Christ, we believe that we shall also live with him. For we know that Christ being raised from the dead will never die again; death no longer has dominion over him. The death he died he died to sin, once for all, but the life he lives he lives to God. So you also must consider yourselves dead to sin and alive to God in Christ Jesus.
>
> Let not sin therefore reign in your mortal bodies, to make you obey their passions. Do not yield your members to sin as instruments of wickedness, but yield yourselves to God as men who have been brought from death to life, and your members to God as instruments of righteousness. For sin will have no dominion over you, since you are not under law but under grace.

Can we see the impact of what Paul is saying here? He is telling us that if a man is dead, he is free from sin. To that we would all agree. But at the same time, if we are dead, we will be of no value to Christ's service here on earth. If we could only be dead and alive at the same time, that would solve our dilemma. Surely that is quite unthinkable, we retort! Yet it is right here that Paul makes a startling statement. He lays down the principle that because of our union with Christ, whereby we have been made one with him, we have shared in our Lord's death on the cross. We are to understand that we have actually died with Christ to sin. In a spiritual sense—yet in a very real way—when Christ died on the cross, we died with him. When he gained the victory by his blood, we shared in that victory by death. The rationality behind this is that God sees us as in him. (The concept of "in Christ" is the key to Pauline theology.) What he experienced, we have experienced. So we are dead. As a result, we are free from sin's dominion over us. It is no longer our master; our "old man" has been crucified with Christ (Gal. 2:20). Furthermore, not only have we died with Christ and shared in that experience of death, but because we are in him we have also been spiritually resurrected with him. We live because he lives. We are now animated by the resurrected life of our Lord in the person of his Holy Spirit. Can sin thus lord it over us? It absolutely cannot! We are dead to it and alive to God.

We recognize that this truth does not appeal to one's human logic. It is most difficult to realize these truths as we look at our real selves. Yet God says it is true, and by faith we accept it. In actuality, it is only faith that can grasp this tremendous reality. But therein lies victory. As one author has pointedly expressed it:

> When Christ died on the cross to sin, we were identified with Him in that death to sin. That is we died with Him. By our union with Him in His death, we were freed from the penalty of sin and emancipated from the power of sin. All our sanctification therefore must be traced to, and rests upon, the atoning sacrifice of our Lord Jesus Christ. The cross of Christ is the efficient cause of deliverance from the power of sin. Freedom from the dominion of sin is a blessing we may claim by faith, just as we accept pardon.[2]

Here is how this principle works in everyday experience: Let us say we are met by one of our old weaknesses. We have striven to overcome it but with little success. Now, however, we realize our identification with Christ in his death and resurrection and by faith in that fact we say, "This sin has no more power over me. I am dead to it." Then in faith we look to God alone for the victory, and the resurrected life (the Holy Spirit) within us gives complete victory over the temptation. Faith in the fact of our death to sin and vital look of faith to God is the answer. Thus, we live in a new freedom never before experienced. Faith is the victory that overcomes the world. Not only in eternity are we delivered from the penalty and presence of sin, but by faith we are saved from its daily power. Our battle is to stay on the ground of faith.

This is what it means to live a holy life; we walk in actual fellowship with the living Christ, daily being cleansed when we err but exercising constant faith in our identification with him and looking to him we achieve victory. He resides within us, and we are in him. He simply lives his life through us. And that quality of life cannot be anything but powerful in Christian mission, for it is not our life as such, it is Christ's life that is manifest. This is a marvellous truth! And it can be an experiential reality for all Christians. This leads us to discuss the resource that is ours in the Spirit of God.

The Power of the Holy Spirit

The work of the Holy Spirit must be seen for our immediate purposes in a two-fold sense. First, God imparts the person and power of the Holy Spirit to the believer to make his life holy. One simply cannot live a holy life apart from the Holy Spirit. This we have already mentioned. Second, it is the purpose of the Holy Spirit to demonstrate his power through the believer, thus making Christian service effective and fruitful. As R. A. Torrey has correctly pointed out:

> The Holy Spirit is the person who imparts to the individual believer

> the power that belongs to God. This is the Holy Spirit's work in the believer, to take what belongs to God and make it ours. All the manifold power of God belongs to the children of God as their birthright in Christ becomes ours in actual and experimental possession through the Holy Spirit's work in us as individuals. To the extent that we understand and claim for ourselves the Holy Spirit's work, to that extent do we obtain for ourselves the fullness of power in Christian life and service that God has provided for us in Christ.[3]

If one is to be effective in mission, one must be properly related to the Holy Spirit. What then is the scriptural principle of our relationship to the Spirit of God? How can we relate ourselves to him so that he will give us power to live and serve Christ successfully?

Let it first be said that all believers are indwelt by the Holy Spirit and sealed by his stamp. This is clear from the New Testament. But the Scriptures also made it abundantly clear that Christians are also to be filled with the Holy Spirit. A believer is not merely a possessor of the Spirit, he is to be filled with the Spirit as well. This is that relationship with God's Spirit that makes service powerful. This is forcefully brought out in the following passages of Scripture:

> And behold, I send the promise of my Father upon you; but stay in the city, until you are clothed with power from on high (Luke 24:49).
>
> But you shall receive power when the Holy Spirit has come upon you; and you shall be my witnesses in Jerusalem and in all Judea and Samaria and to the end of the earth (Acts 1:8).
>
> And they were all filled with the Holy Spirit and began to speak in other tongues, as the Spirit gave them utterance (Acts 2:4).
>
> And when they had prayed, the place in which they were gathered together was shaken; and they were all filled with the Holy Spirit and spoke the word of God with boldness (Acts 4:31).
>
> And do not get drunk with wine, for that is debauchery; but be filled with the Spirit (Eph. 5:18).

Besides this tremendous weight of the Scriptures—and there are many other passages—effective men of God give testimony to the validity of the concept of the Spirit-filled life. For example, R. A. Torrey said, "I was led to seek the baptism [filling] with the Holy

Spirit, because I became convinced from the study of the Acts of the Apostles that no one had a right to preach the gospel until he had." Charles G. Finney wrote, "I was powerfully converted on the morning of the 10th of October, 1821. In the evening of the same day I received overwhelming baptisms [infillings] of the Holy Ghost." A. T. Pierson said concerning his ministry after having been filled with the Spirit, "I have seen more conversion and accomplished more in eighteen months since I received that blessing than in the eighteen years previous."

How does one receive the fullness of the Spirit and walk in his daily anointing? One must first confess and forsake all of his known sins. As much as we can know, we must be cleansed by the blood of Christ (1 John 1:9). This principle has been made clear. Then, one must surrender himself without reservation to Jesus Christ as Lord of life (Rom. 12:1-2). Finally, one should pray and simply trust God to do the work of filling (Luke 11:13). It is that simple. The very moment we confess all known sins (we all have unknown sins and can hardly confess these), surrender totally to Christ and trust God to fill us with his Spirit, he will surely meet our need and we will become a Spirit-filled Christian. Simple, yet profound!

There is obviously a definite relationship between being filled with the Spirit and walking daily with Christ. Being filled with the Spirit is not a once-for-all experience as is the case concerning conversion. It is not something that brings one into a state of perfection as some teach. And there is not one particular "gift of the Spirit" one must receive to know he has been filled. It is not necessarily even an emotional experience. The point is, being filled with the Spirit is something we need each day we live. As someone has said, we are "leaky vessels," and we need to be refilled every day. This is why Paul said in Ephesians 5:8 (literally) "continue to be filled with the Spirit." So, as we walk moment by moment with Christ, we daily come to him as empty vessels to a full fountain to have our cup made full and running over with his Spirit. If we fail to walk with Christ, we will fail to come to him for the divine infilling of his Holy Spirit, and we are thus impotent in his service, and we lose the conscious glow of Christ's presence. To walk with God, therefore, is to walk in the continual infilling of his power. When this is one's perpetual experience, he is bound to exemplify the power of a holy life, and the dynamic of the Holy Spirit will work through him to make his service effective.

Furthermore, when we walk in the Holy Spirit's fullness many promises of the Scriptures can be claimed:

> In the Holy Spirit we are set free from the law of sin and death (Rom. 8:2).
> In the Holy Spirit we are strengthened in the inward man (Eph. 3:16).
> In the Holy Spirit we find God's leading (Rom. 8:14).
> In the Holy Spirit we bear fruit (Gal. 5:22-23).
> In the Holy Spirit we are led into all truth (John 16:13).
> In the Holy Spirit we learn to pray effectively (Eph. 6:18).
> In the Holy Spirit we can communicate the truth to others (1 Cor. 2:15).
> In the Holy Spirit we can evangelize in power (Acts 2:4-41).

It can be concluded that apart from a vital relationship to the Spirit of God, one can hope for little magnetism about his life or little power in his ministry. We simply cannot evangelize without the Spirit's working through us toward the unbelieving. A proper relationship with the Spirit of God is vital for mission. Also, it is the Holy Spirit who inspires the evangelistic passion within us.

The Power of a Holy Passion

David Brainerd, the great missionary to the American Indians, said, "I cared not where or how I lived or what hardships I went through so that I could but gain souls for Christ. While I was asleep I dreamed of these things, and when I awoke the first thing I thought of was this great work. All of my desire was for the conversion of the heathen and all my hope was in God." In a similar spirit Thomas Chalmers prayed, "Recall the twenty-one years of my service; give me back its shipwreck, give me its standings in the face of death, give me it surrounded by fierce savages with spears and clubs, give it back to me with clubs knocking me down, give all this back to me, and I will be your missionary still."

This is the attitude God honors. This is the kind of passion that communicates to people. As John Wesley is reported saying, "Get on fire for God and people will come to watch you burn." Of course, I do not refer to a shallow vociferous approach, but trying to "play it cool" in reaching men for Christ can be most damaging to evangelistic outreach. God desires his evangelists to be burdened, concerned, enthusiastic, and zealous to spread the good news to the millions who desperately need to hear the message. And this attitude the Holy Spirit will instill as we seek his strength, wisdom, and compassion. One would hope that all Christians could become so committed to the evangelistic task that such a passion would grip the entire church. If this situation is ever to happen, I suppose it must first begin with the pastor-evangelist.

The Power of Prayer

Prayer is another tremendous resource of power about which little perhaps need be said here. It is not that the theme is in any sense secondary. On the contrary, it is vital. The reason for saying little here is that so much fine material has already been produced on the subject that anything this author could contribute would be of little additional value. Let it be said simply that prayer is essential to spiritual power in one's life and ministry. We get what we claim by faith in prayer. Every great spiritual movement has been conceived, born, and matured in intercession. Whether it be Jacob, centuries ago, wrestling in prayer by the river Jabbok or the recent revival that has come to many parts of the world; through the millennia of God's dealings with men prayer has been the key that opened the treasure house of God's power. Probably one of our basic problems today is that "you have not because you ask not" (Jas. 4:2). This we know. The issue is that we begin to pray and lead the entire church to pray. Renewal and effective evangelism wait on the power of prayer. It is a vast resource for all Christians.

The Power of the Word of God

The "good seed" that falls in the ground and brings forth fruit is the word of God. And it is a word of power: "Is not my word like fire, says the Lord, and like a hammer which breaks the rock in pieces?" (Jer. 23:29). Space precludes an excursion into the interesting and relevant theological field of revelation and inspiration. What is important to realize is that the Christian has tremendous resources in the power of our message. As Paul said, "I am not ashamed of the gospel: it is the power of God for salvation to every one who has faith" (Rom. 1:16).

The Bible itself has much to say about the power of the word in the hands of the Holy Spirit.

> It is the instrument of the Spirit in conversion (Jas. 1:8).
> It produces faith (Rom. 10:17).
> It is the means of cleansing (Eph. 5:25-26).
> It is that which builds one up in Christ (Acts 20:32).
> It is a source of wisdom (Ps. 119:130).
> It gives the assurance of eternal life (1 John 5:13).

These realities were brought home to me on an occasion when a pastor friend was speaking to a high school group. After faithfully presenting the gospel, at the conclusion of his message he quoted that word of Paul in 2 Corinthians 6:2: "Behold, now is the day of salvation." As the group was leaving, a young man came to him and said, "I had no intention of giving myself to Christ, but when you said now is the day of salvation, it really hit me. I want to become a Christian now." Truly "the word of God is living and active, sharper than any two-edged sword" (Heb. 4:12).

The Christian who desires to win others should realize he has a most powerful weapon in this warfare. He can unashamedly and positively present the good news in the full assurance that God will honor his word of power and use it to speak to the hearts of the hearers. The proclaimer honors God when he honors God's word by forthrightly in faith declaring it. This is why we spent time discussing the basic *kerygma,* for that is the message God's Spirit uses to bring men to faith in Christ. One need not rely on human wisdom and ingenuity. As a matter of fact, if he does, he forsakes the great source of genuine power that is at his disposal. The word of God alone is the sword of the Spirit (Eph. 6:17).

In the final analysis, it is probably correct to sum it all up by emphasizing the resource in one's life of surrender to Jesus Christ.

The Power of a Committed Life

God's action through the life of the Christian waits for that life to be surrendered to his will and purpose. Knowledge comes through committal (John 7:17); prayer is dependent upon a surrendered will (1 John 3:22); one's joy and winsome testimony is based on a yieldedness to God's authority (John 15:10-11), and the Holy Spirit empowers only those who present themselves unreservedly to God's desire (Acts 5:32).

Even the secular psychologists tell us of the unifying influence and powerful impact of being committed to a great cause. The world longs to see those who are committed—committed to God and the evangelization of the world. Moreover, the mission task that God lays upon his people is such that only the resource and power of a deep committal will see it accomplished. May God bring us all into that kind of surrender to himself and to our task to bring Christ to all. The world waits!

Notes

1. Gavin Reid, op. cit., p. 57.
2. Steven Barabas, *So Great Salvation* (New York: Fleming H. Revell), pp. 88-9.
3. R. A. Torrey, *How to Obtain Fullness of Power* (London: Lakeland Paperbacks, 1955), p. 31.

Appendix
A Church Survey

Perhaps as never before the church needs to take a fresh look at itself. This need can motivate a local church to conduct a "diagnostic survey" of itself. The purpose of such a survey is to evaluate objectively the life of a local church in order that its ministry and witness may become more effective. All sincere Christians surely desire to see the life and ministry of their church enhanced, but before this happens it may be essential to "overhaul" aspects of the present church program. Such an undertaking calls for objectivity, honesty, and not a little bravery. The outline that follows will provide in broad terms some guidelines for conducting such a survey. It seems clear that if we can come to understand just where we are in local church life, we can see more clearly where we need to go.

I. The Setting of Goals or Aims

In setting goals, ask these questions:

1. What is the essential mission of the church, and how does it relate to our local church?

2. How should this mission affect the aims and plans of our local church, and does it actually do so?

3. What should be, therefore, the aims of our local church?

4. Are the church members conscious of these aims?

5. Do these aims govern the development of the church program and the organizations and their functions? If not, why?

II. Surveying the Community

1. Prepare a map of the community, indicating by a colored line

the area surrounding the church. (Show church location.)

2. Prepare a description of the church's area of responsibility; e.g. location, type of housing, age, industrial or residential, racial patterns, subcultural groups, institutions, problems related to its environment, etc. This will take some study.

3. Describe the community needs that should be met by the church.

4. Evaluate the effectiveness of the church in meeting the needs of its immediate community. What can and should be done to meet these needs?

III. Surveying the Organizational Life of the Church

General

1. Summarize briefly the history of the church and how this relates (if it does) to the present church life.

2. Evaluate and criticize the church's constitution and/or by-laws if it has any.

3. Study the church property and buildings. What long- (or short-) term plans should be made by the church concerning its location and future building needs? How adequate are the present buildings to meet the needs of the community? What repairs or changes or building plans are vital for the present and future? Are we using the present building to the best advantage in accordance with the church's message and ministry? What other building resources are available?

Worship

1. What is the program of church music? Is this vital aspect of church life given proper interest and work?

2. Study the church services of worship. Are they relevant? Is the language used that which communicates? Are the church ordinances meaningfully observed? What is being done to educate in worship? Are the services "alive"? What can be done? What should

be kept? Do we understand the relationship between worship and mission?

Evangelism and World Missions

Describe the outreach of the church. What is actually being done now? Is there an evangelistic committee? What is the record of successful outreach over the past ten years? Are the church organizations involved in evangelism? How conscious are the church members of the need and centrality of evangelism? Are the worship services effectively evangelistic? How can we reach outsiders? What training is given members? How can we be more relevant to different groups of people in the community? What are we doing in worldwide evangelization?

Pastoral Care

1. How are members received into the church? What does the church do to integrate new members into the total church program? What plans are there for conserving and training new members in the Christian life and church life? How adequate and useful are the membership rolls? What action is taken over inactive members?

2. Evaluate church ministries. What services are rendered to family life—before and after marriage? What about the church's "crisis" ministry, i.e. in times of death, serious illness, birth? What about the problems of broken families, delinquency, crime, when these occur in the life of the church members or in the community? To what extent is the whole church involved in pastoral care?

Christian Education

Evaluate the overall effectiveness of the church's educational program. This should include the work of the Sunday School, women's work, men's organizations, etc. These questions must be asked: Is our church truly educating people in the Bible? Is there any segment of the membership not receiving teaching in the Scriptures? If so, what can be done? Are organizations in line with the mission? Is there a leadership training program? Is the laity being taught and equipped for ministry? Are all given an opportunity to exercise their gifts of the Spirit?

Stewardship

Study the church plan for promoting and practicing Christian stewardship. Describe and evaluate the plan of church finance. What emphasis is placed on this important aspect of dedication? What portion of the membership gives regularly? What is done to increase this number? How badly hindered is the life and ministry of the church because of poor stewardship? Is there a reluctance to emphasize stewardship? How about a stewardship campaign? Does the church spend its monies in such a way as to encourage giving?

Recreational and Social Ministries

Evaluate church recreation, for old and young, and other specialized activities, e.g. drama, youth clubs, holiday clubs. What sort of impact is the church making on the community? What social needs exist? How can the church help to meet these needs?

Leadership

Evaluate leadership participation. What proportion of church members have some definite place of service in the church program? In the light of the study of the church organizations, how adequate is the church leadership? How are leaders discovered? What training, if any, do they receive to do their job effectively?

Administrative

1. Study the problem of coordination and correlation. Is the church well integrated? How do the organizations relate to one another and help one another? Is the leadership of the church's total program unified and harmonious? Are there "churches within the church"?

Are there too many overlappings and duplications of activities and functions? Do all of the organizations live, minister, develop, function, and serve in the light of the mission of the church? Is there any overall group coordinating the whole church life? Is too much power vested in a few?

2. Study the administrative facilities of the church. Is there adequate equipment, e.g. duplicators, typewriters, etc.? Does the pastor do an unfair amount of this work? Could the load be shared by others? Are good records kept? Are they used and found helpful to a better church life?

Public Relations

Study and evaluate the promotional and publicity plans of the church. Are the monies used wisely and effectively? Do these plans "grab" people in their interest, i.e. do they truly communicate?

IV. Surveying the Church Leadership

In surveying the church leaders be sure to maintain a spirit of understanding and patience; people are often sensitive here.

Interviewing the pastor. How does the minister see his role? How did he face the problem of getting started in the church? How does he cope with the problems of relationships with staff and church members? How does he feel about the need of church administration? How does he feel about the evangelistic enterprise? What does the pastor consider his primary function in the life of the church? Is he able to fulfill that role? If not, why not? What plan does he have to find time for leisure and for his family? What would he like to see changed in the church?

Interviewing the official body (deacons, stewards, elders, etc.). How do they see their role? What do they consider to be their relationship to the pastor and church? What are their particular problems? What do they feel hinders the life and effectiveness of the church? Are their attitudes in line with the New Testament?

Interviewing the church lay-leaders. What do they feel is their role in the life of the church? Do they feel they were properly enlisted? Do they feel they are receiving proper training for their tasks? How do they feel about the specific organization in which they serve? Do they feel overworked with too many responsibilities?

It is well to interview at random a few representative lay-members (such as a young person, an old person, even children) to get something of the reaction of the average person who comes but takes no active part in leadership. Do they feel everything is done by the few? Is it so? Do they feel mere spectators? What would they like changed?

Summary and Suggestions

It is obvious that the purpose of such an extensive survey is the assessment of the total church life. All of the organizations will have to be looked at in depth and evaluated. Perhaps an analogy could be found in an extensive physical examination that a doctor would carry out on a patient for the purpose of diagnosing ills so that the proper remedy may be found. This undertaking must be the work of several. Perhaps a group of the key leaders in the church would be the logical ones to do the work. As already emphasized, it must be done with objectivity, honesty, bravery, and above all, in the spirit of helpfulness, understanding, and love. Much discussion and prayer must go into the venture. The whole idea is for a local church to understand itself in the light of the great mission of the church and to attempt to bring itself and all of its activities in line with that mission on the basis of total lay involvement, serving on the principle of exercising their spiritual gifts.

Moreover, such a survey must not be just put on paper and laid to rest. It should form a working plan to change and update the whole life of the church. In the end it would be hoped that God's Spirit will so lead in the matter that his blessings will result in a far more effective ministry for the church and many more won to

Christ and his kingdom. Granted, the church survey is the negative diagnostic side. Now the church must build a great new program to the glory of God. That is the positive side each local church must undertake. But the rewards are well worth the extensive effort.